IN PURSUIT OF HAPPINESS

KNOWING WHAT YOU WANT
GETTING WHAT YOU NEED

BY

E. PERRY GOOD

Designed and Illustrated by

JEFFREY HALE

❖

New View Publications
Chapel Hill

This book is for Jessica Good,
Margot Hale and Nicholas Hale.

Sixth printing 1994

Design and illustrations by Jeffrey Hale.

Typography by Charles Fennimore, Desktop Publishing, Inc.

Library of Congress Cataloging-in-Publication Data
Good, E. Perry, 1943-
    In Pursuit of Happiness
    1. Happiness. 2. Reality Therapy.
I. Title.
BF575.H27G66 1987   158'.1   87-61973
ISBN 0-944337-00-7

Author Speaking Engagements

For information regarding speaking engagements by E. Perry Good, contact the author at P.O. Box 3021, Chapel Hill, N.C. 27515-3021.

Quantity Purchases

Companies, professional groups, clubs, and other organizations may qualify for special terms when ordering quantities of this title. For information contact the Sales Department, New View Publications, P.O. Box 3021, Chapel Hill, N.C. 27515-3021.

Quote from article by Daniel Goleman Copyright © 1986 by The New York Times Company. Reprinted by permission.

Article by Art Buchwald reprinted by permission of the author.

Manufactured in the United States of America.

SPECIAL ACKNOWLEDGEMENT

The ideas in this book are largely based on Dr. William Glasser's work on Reality Therapy and Control Theory. For the past 15 years I have taught these ideas as a Senior Faculty member of the Institute for Reality Therapy. I am grateful for the opportunity to have worked so closely with Dr. Glasser. His constant search for a better understanding of what motivates people and how to help them has been challenging and fascinating. That his ideas work is an understatement. I admire both his simplicity and his tenacity.

Dr. Glasser has been both my teacher and my friend. Without his encouragement and support I might have become a film producer, a politician, or even a bag lady. As it is, I'm making speeches and writing this book on the back of a snail.

I would also like to thank his wife and my friend, Naomi Glasser for her belief in me.

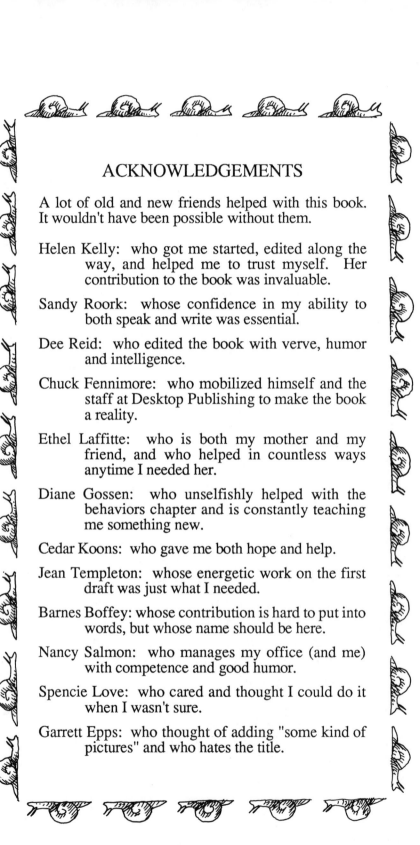

ACKNOWLEDGEMENTS

A lot of old and new friends helped with this book. It wouldn't have been possible without them.

Helen Kelly: who got me started, edited along the way, and helped me to trust myself. Her contribution to the book was invaluable.

Sandy Roork: whose confidence in my ability to both speak and write was essential.

Dee Reid: who edited the book with verve, humor and intelligence.

Chuck Fennimore: who mobilized himself and the staff at Desktop Publishing to make the book a reality.

Ethel Laffitte: who is both my mother and my friend, and who helped in countless ways anytime I needed her.

Diane Gossen: who unselfishly helped with the behaviors chapter and is constantly teaching me something new.

Cedar Koons: who gave me both hope and help.

Jean Templeton: whose energetic work on the first draft was just what I needed.

Barnes Boffey: whose contribution is hard to put into words, but whose name should be here.

Nancy Salmon: who manages my office (and me) with competence and good humor.

Spencie Love: who cared and thought I could do it when I wasn't sure.

Garrett Epps: who thought of adding "some kind of pictures" and who hates the title.

We want to thank these people
who put up with us, helped us,
and most of all remained
enthusiastic about what we
were doing.

Jessica Good
Fred Good
Anna Dibble

The only freedom which deserves the name is that of pursuing our own good in our own way, so long as we do not attempt to deprive others of theirs, or impede their efforts to obtain it.

— John Stuart Mill

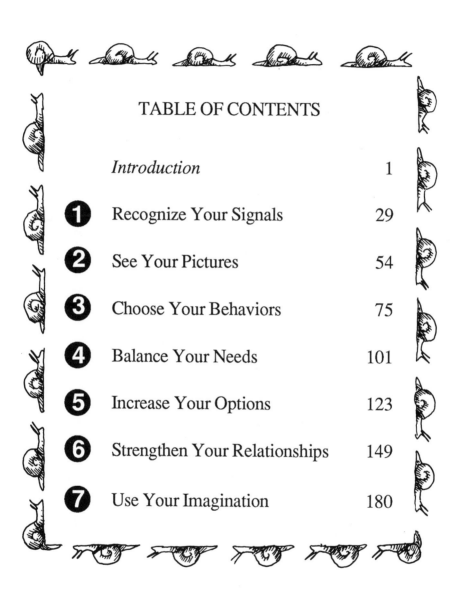

TABLE OF CONTENTS

It's risky to write a book about happiness. Happiness is out of style. Happiness is superficial. Happiness is for little kids. Happiness is not serious enough for anyone over the age of twelve. And yet, our forefathers (and mothers) thought it was serious enough to include in the Declaration of Independence:

We hold these truths to be self-evident, that all men are created equal, that they are endowed by their Creator with certain unalienable Rights, that among these are Life, Liberty and the Pursuit of Happiness.

In America, the pursuit of happiness is an inalienable right. That means that everyone has the right to pursue it. The problem is HOW. Every day we are offered countless suggestions about what will bring happiness: a sausage biscuit in the morning, a beer after work, a telephone call, the right soft drink, or even a certain soap powder. Advertisers rarely talk about the cost of their products. They know that if they can convince you that their product will make you happier, you will buy it if you can. Some people think therapy can bring happiness. Others think drugs or alcohol are the answer.

So you find yourself asking:

• What is happiness?

• How do I find it?

• Will I know when I have it?

• Does anyone ever find it?

• Is there a way to pursue it that I can understand?

• Are therapists the only people who can help me find happiness?

• Can drugs make me happy?

2

Happiness is a by-product of leading a balanced, varied and satisfying life which meets your needs.

If you observe a really happy man (or woman) you will find him building a boat, writing a symphony, educating his daughter, growing double dahlias in his garden or looking for dinosaur eggs in the Gobi Desert. He will not be searching for happiness as if it were a collar button that has rolled under the radiator. He will not be striving for it as a goal in itself.

– W. B. Wolfe

Happiness is NOT something you can look for and find.

BUT you can begin to understand what to aim for and what actions to take in your life in order to be happier. If you are aiming in the right direction for YOU, you will be happier with your life. Essentially, then, you will be pursuing happiness.

The direction in which your life is going is directly related to whether happiness will be a by-product of what you are doing.

Your own pursuit of happiness, then, depends upon knowing what you want and distinguishing between what you WANT and what you honestly NEED to be happy. Some of what you WANT may not be what you NEED for a balanced, varied and satisfying life.

Since it is not possible to just make yourself feel happier, whether you are happy depends upon what you are DOING and THINKING.

A FRAME OF REFERENCE

It's easier to think about your life and what you are doing with it if you have a frame of reference. You may not have a clear way to think about what motivates you and those around you. The easily understood and straightforward frame of reference used in this book is that you have basic needs which must be satisfied if you are going to be happy. These needs are both mental and physical. You are born with them and are driven to meet them.

Simply put:

If you meet these needs you are happy. If you don't, you are unhappy.

This sounds simple. But it's not THAT simple.

Meeting these needs is harder than it sounds because you meet your needs through yourself and others. As you have found out by living, any time another person is involved it is difficult to get both what you want and what the other person wants.

You have basic needs, and so does everyone else.

Complications occur when the way you want to meet your needs with another person doesn't match the way that person wants to meet theirs. For example, this kind of mismatch could occur with your husband over something as simple as what to have for dinner (you love Mexican, he hates it) to something as complicated as how to raise your children (you're strict, he's not).

WHAT
ARE
MY
BASIC
NEEDS
?

Your basic needs are:

LOVE

Belonging • Friendship • Caring • Involvement

POWER

Importance • Recognition • Skill • Competence

FUN

Pleasure • Enjoyment • Learning • Laughter

FREEDOM

Choice • Independence • Liberty • Autonomy

YOU HAVE MENTAL
AND PHYSICAL NEEDS

Obviously, you have basic physical needs – food, shelter, clothing and water. You probably pay attention to those. But do you realize that you have mental needs that are equally important?

You hear the word "needs" all the time. Psychologists say, "We all have needs." Your depressed friend Jane might say, "I need chocolate!" But you have probably never known what your needs REALLY are, or whether meeting your needs has anything to do with your present state of happiness or misery.

Now you KNOW what your needs are. And yes, they have a lot to do with whether you are happy or miserable.

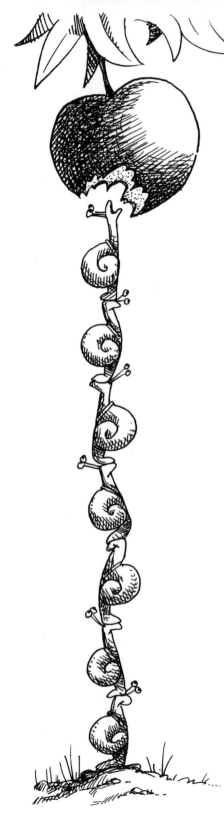

HOW DID THESE NEEDS DEVELOP?

Our basic needs developed very early in the history of women and men. In order to survive, our most primitive ancestors had to both cooperate and compete. They had to compete for everything from getting the biggest piece of meat to the warmest place by the fire. At the same time, they had to cooperate with each other enough to remain part of the group. They couldn't just check into the Holiday Inn when they weren't getting along.

Over time, cooperating developed their needs for LOVE and FUN just as competing developed their needs for POWER and FREEDOM.

Those who achieved a balance between cooperating and competing were the survivors because they could both depend on the group and depend on themselves. This is still true today.

10

THE NEW YORK TIMES

An article in the *New York Times* by Daniel Goleman entitled "The Strange Agony of Success" (August 24, 1986) makes a strong case for balance as an answer for many young professionals who succeed only to find that they are disappointed and even emotionally damaged by their career climb.

> . . . *but in these high-pressure, high reward jobs, particularly those on Wall Street, in corporate law, the computer industry and in the world of the entrepreneur, psychotherapists say that many executives soon lose all sense of balance between their work and the other aspects of their lives. And that is an important loss: As Sigmund Freud said, the two hallmarks of a healthy maturity are the capacities to love and to work.*

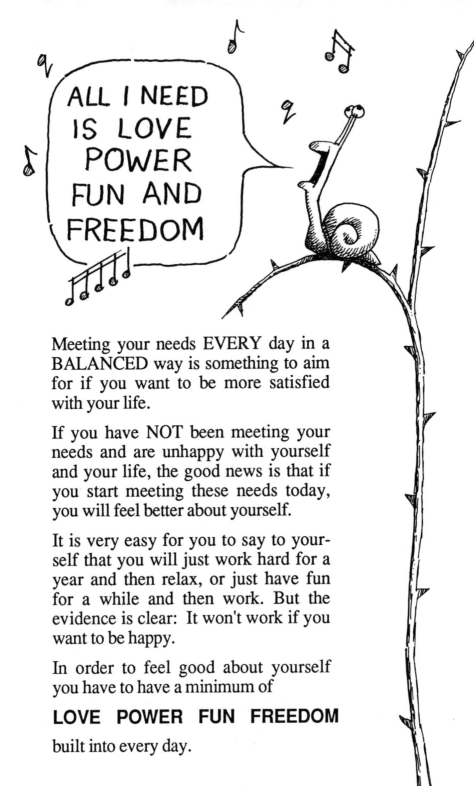

ALL I NEED
IS LOVE
POWER
FUN AND
FREEDOM

Meeting your needs EVERY day in a
BALANCED way is something to aim
for if you want to be more satisfied
with your life.

If you have NOT been meeting your
needs and are unhappy with yourself
and your life, the good news is that if
you start meeting these needs today,
you will feel better about yourself.

It is very easy for you to say to yourself that you will just work hard for a
year and then relax, or just have fun
for a while and then work. But the
evidence is clear: It won't work if you
want to be happy.

In order to feel good about yourself
you have to have a minimum of

LOVE POWER FUN FREEDOM

built into every day.

12

Us laughs, us sings, us brings flower bouquets, all to be loved.   – Alice Walker *The Color Purple*

Let's talk about love and belonging in the modern world. It is certainly a topic that gets a lot of press. Husbands and wives, friends and lovers, parents and children, families and friends, bosses and employees all read, talk, fight and fantasize about this influential need.

Your ancestors needed it to survive. So do you. Everyone has a different notion about love. You may complain that "you can't live with it, and you can't live without it."

Love means belonging. You meet your need for it in both your intimate and friendly relationships. Your spouse, family members, boy or girl friends, and close pals are all sources of love as well as recipients of the love you have to give. Other relationships in your life – with people you meet at work, groups to which you belong, people who help you (doctors, therapists, social workers, ministers), neighbors who are special, and teams on which you play – all provide ways to satisfy your need to belong.

This need for love and belonging is so strong that you might endure some pretty terrible treatment just to have what you believe is love from another person.

For example, consider the teenage girl who entered a runaway shelter with terrible cuts and abrasions all over her face. Her mother had beaten her with a high-heeled shoe. Yet within a few hours the teenager ran away from the shelter and went home. The fear of having no love from her mother was stronger than the fear of being beaten again.

Many adults remain in destructive relationships through repeated painful incidents – beatings, arguments, threats and sexual abuse – for fear they will have no love if they leave. "Love" at its worst is frequently seen as better than no love at all.

But what you need in order to survive and be a satisfied person is a better kind of love. You need love that creates in you a deep and true sense that there is someone who cares about you and whom you care about.

In order for you to have this kind of love you have to first love and care about yourself. You have probably heard "love yourself" before and wondered exactly how to do this. The way to love yourself is to meet your basic needs in ways that YOU ideally want to meet them, and in ways that won't hurt you and others. Learning how to do this takes some knowledge and some practice.

YOU NEED LOVE

Everyone has, inside himself . . . what shall I call it? A piece of good news! Everyone is . . . a very great, very important character.

— Ugto Betti *The Burnt Flower Bed*

In addition to love, you also need power — a sense of importance. Power is not something that most people will admit they need or want. You probably get a little nervous at the mention of power. Power is not popular because you often think of it in its most negative forms: power over other people, power that robs others of what they need. This is power gone awry.

Any of your needs can be satisfied, at least temporarily, in negative, ineffective ways.

But there are need-satisfying ways to gain power that are positive and do not keep others from meeting their needs.

One way to meet your need for power is to receive recognition.

This is probably available to you each day in the work you do at home or in a workplace. Promotions, awards, good grades and praise go a long way in enhancing your sense of power.

You can also give yourself recognition. I sometimes give myself a pat on the back when I make a delicious dessert without a recipe. You may not have thought of giving yourself credit, because it seems egotistical. Actually, it's essential if you are going to be happy with yourself and your life.

You can also meet your need for power by being in charge – of people, projects or just yourself. Good grades in school can give you power. Competing with others is another way to achieve power. Sports give a great sense of power to the competitors. The coach of the football team has power, win or lose.

You meet your need for power, too, when you gain respect from yourself or others. Perhaps you resist temptation, finish a particularly difficult task, or lose 10 pounds. You feel a sense of achievement, of power. Others offer you respect when they see you being effective and successful in your life.

Your opinions are valued. You have an impact on other people. Nothing can destroy a marriage or any relationship as quickly as a lack of respect for the other person's thoughts or feelings. Each of us must have that need-fulfilling sense of importance, of believing that what we want is recognized.

YOU NEED POWER

Fun is what you do when you don't have to do it.
— Mark Twain

The Puritan influence on our culture has helped destroy the notion that having fun is acceptable behavior. Many people believe that fun is just for young kids and that anyone else who has too much fun is, well, immoral. This is another of our needs that is misunderstood.

Our ancestors learned to enjoy human contact in many ways. As they lived and worked so closely, the need for tension release was high. Games, food, rituals, music, stories and jokes helped our ancestors live together more harmoniously. Without such fun, they might have just killed each other off during a long, cold winter.

Most adults find it hard to believe that fun is a basic need. You may believe that fun is what you do when you have finished everything else you have to do. You may not see that fun makes your life brighter. When I was a teenager I was very active in the church my family attended. We used to travel around the state going to meetings and having a wonderful time. My brother, who did not equate fun with church work, told my mother that I was getting away with murder in the name of the church.

One of the problems with trying to meet your need for fun is that you may think you have to do something wild to have fun. Not true: Fun comes in many forms. Think of fun as pleasure. Fun doesn't have to mean dancing all night (but it could). Fun could be an evening walk with your dog, or paying the toll for the car behind you at the toll booth. Anything that gives you pleasure without hurting someone else can be fun.

Fun is a need that children are especially good at meeting because they have the freedom to play. Play is an important source of learning – for children and adults. Children usually think learning is fun, until they get to school – then it becomes work. If you are having a hard time thinking of learning as fun, try to recall the FIRST time you learned to ride a bicycle, say your ABCs or put together a jigsaw puzzle. Did any of those experiences create a kind of "ah-ha" moment that made you want to smile, giggle or shout for joy? You were having fun!

When you use your mind in a spontaneous way, you meet your need for fun. You tell a joke. You laugh. You say something silly. You let your mind go out to play. And, in the process, you either learn something or discover some of your own creativity. That kind of fun is what has kept our species alive. Other kinds of fun can add immeasurably to your happiness.

YOU NEED FUN

Is freedom anything but the right to live as we wish?

                         –Epictetus

If you don't have the freedom to make choices and gain some amount of control over your life, then you cannot meet your other basic needs.

Your need for freedom is satisfied through the choices you make. The ability to make small and large choices for yourself is a freedom you might take for granted. I was reminded of just how much freedom I have in my life when my daughter said to me, "Mom, when I'm grown up, I can do anything I want to, can't I?" From her point of view, as a child whose freedom is limited by adult rules and school schedules, the freedom of being grown up seems awesome. And it is! As an adult you have the freedom to make decisions about your life. You also make decisions that will affect others' lives. That's wonderful, and it is a little scary. Too much freedom can interfere with your meeting other needs, especially belonging and achievement.

Learning to use freedom to make wise choices about the people, situations and places in your life is a big task. It's hard to know what will help satisfy our needs and what will hurt us or others. Allowing yourself the freedom to meet your needs can be exhilarating. When you allow yourself the freedom to meet your needs, you meet your need for freedom! That means allowing yourself to want what you want, to go for it (as long as you are not interfering with others meeting their needs).

Remember that you can be your own worst enemy when it comes to limiting yourself. When you limit yourself, you are NOT meeting your need for freedom. But knowing what you have is often less scary than not knowing what you might get. That is why, for example, many people stay in bad marriages or in dead-end jobs. They are miserable, but at least they know what they have.

Your need for freedom is deep. Your need for autonomy, for the ability to make choices in your life, is strong. If you have heard a 2-year-old say, "I do it myself!" you have seen the need for freedom. If you have ever punched a time clock you have felt the need for freedom. If you have ever had someone try to control you with feelings, you have felt the need for freedom. For example, a parent might interfere with your need for freedom by saying, "You never come visit your old father anymore."

When you do not make choices, or when you forget about this need, then you do not feel happy with your life.

YOU NEED FREEDOM

YOU HAVE CHOICES

Even though your basic needs are the same, there are many choices you can make about how you want to meet those needs.

This is what makes you unique. No other person will ever meet his or her needs in exactly the same way that you will meet yours. You have ideal

pictures of how you want to meet your needs and you have a complex behavioral system that helps you get what you want.

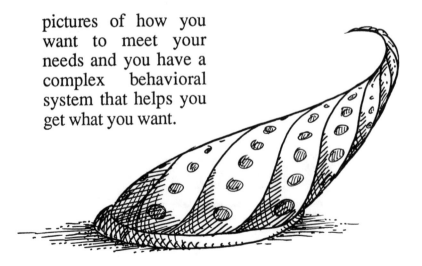

DON'T FORGET

In everything you do, you are either meeting your needs or you are not. Whether or not you realize it, you are deciding about your life every moment of the day or night. Learning to make the choices that will effectively meet your needs is a key to the pursuit of happiness.

In other words, if you don't make a decision, then you have made a decision. Nothing will change in your life if you don't do something different from what you have been doing.

Sometimes you don't make decisions or take action because you are not sure of yourself. You are not sure exactly what to do, or what to aim for. You are not sure how to even begin to increase balance and variety in your life.

SOMETHING TO AIM FOR

This book is divided into seven sections or TARGETS.

1 RECOGNIZE YOUR SIGNALS

2 SEE YOUR PICTURES

3 CHOOSE YOUR BEHAVIORS

4 BALANCE YOUR NEEDS

5 INCREASE YOUR OPTIONS

6 STRENGTHEN YOUR RELATIONSHIPS

7 USE YOUR IMAGINATION

These seven targets are designed to give you a way to think about how you are meeting your needs as well as some actions to take that will help you find more balance and satisfaction in your life.

Although it is easiest to think of these targets separately, they build on each other. The best way to improve your aim is to start at the beginning. Then after you're comfortable with the ideas in the first target move on to the next one.

TARGETS IN YOUR
PURSUIT OF HAPPINESS

These sections are simply targets in your pursuit of happiness. You've heard the old expression:

shooting in the dark

Most of us shoot in the dark when we try to make our lives better and happier, knowing that we should try to do better in our relationships with others and ourselves but not always knowing where to aim.

This book will help you learn how to recognize your signals, see your pictures, balance your needs, choose your behaviors, satisfy conflicting needs, strengthen your relationships and use your creativity to get more of what you want.

You won't always hit the bull's-eye, and sometimes you may even miss the target completely. But knowing that you're aiming in the right direction is worth a lot.

In each of the following TARGETS there will be a THINK IT section and a DO IT section.

The reason for the THINK IT section is very simple. If you understand the principles behind the targets and you are able to THINK about them, you will be more able to DO the DO IT section.

If you do not understand or know the basic principles behind the actions you take, it is difficult to change your life for the better. And you won't have much of a chance of being happy.

The DO IT section of each target will be the most difficult, because in this part you will be asked to take action. You will be asked to DO something different from what you have been doing.

The only way to meet your needs in the long run is by doing something. You must act to get what you want.

You would probably agree that you can't think yourself thin. Reading diet books and worrying about fat will not help you lose weight unless you do the diet and exercise. If thinking about being thin could make you thin, I would have disappeared years ago.

Reading and worrying and being depressed might help for a little while, but to get what you want, you have to DO something.

You cannot just think and feel to be happier.

SIGNALS

❶ RECOGNIZE YOUR SIGNALS

You have your own personal survival system.

It is made up of many different types of internal alarms.

Understanding these signals can make your life happier.

These internal alarms are directly related to your basic needs.

The signals which make up your survival system can be positive or negative. They tell you immediately and accurately whether you are getting what you want.

Some people call these signals "gut feelings," intuitions, or hunches. That's exactly what they are. You may experience them as

*a hollow feeling in
the pit of your stomach
a tightening in your chest
a sensation of pure joy
a flash of anger*

Your internal signals tell you quickly whether you are getting what you want to meet your needs (remember LOVE POWER FUN FREEDOM?). What is happening in your life matches the picture in your mind. You have a picture of a new job in your mind and your boss says, "It's yours!" A MATCH. You get what you want to meet your needs.

WHAT EXACTLY ARE

SIGNALS

Signals are internal sensations which are closely connected with your basic needs and the pictures in your head of how you want your needs met. In fact, without these internal signals you would not know if you were meeting your needs. You would not know if you were happy or miserable.

These signals developed in a primitive part of our early ancestors' brains to let them know if they were getting what they needed to survive. The survivors would notice any differences and quickly determine if those differences would help them or hurt them. Even though your brain is more sophisticated it is still letting you know what you need to survive as well as what you need to be happy.

THINK: WHAT ARE YOUR SIGNALS ABOUT?

WHEN DO SIGNALS OCCUR?

All day long you are experiencing internal signals. Your signals let you know inside yourself when things are very positive (like the pure pleasure you feel when you get a dozen roses for your birthday) or very negative (like the pure pain you feel when your parents say they are getting divorced). You are constantly comparing the pictures that you have in your head of what you want to the pictures that are coming into you from the outside world.

You get an internal signal (positive or negative) and then you think: this IS, or this is NOT, what I want.

Your signals are INTERNAL.

These signals are strong and you usually notice them, even if you don't call them signals. But you also have signals that are not this strong. Call them beeping signals. They're not as loud as a siren but are more like a seat belt beep. They are slightly annoying but don't really jolt you. These signals are no less important than the "louder" signals. They are all a part of your personal survival alarm system.

RECOGNIZE YOUR NEGATIVE SIGNALS

You understand clearly that you have physical needs. Otherwise you wouldn't be alive. Most people don't argue that there is a need for food. You pay attention to the warning signals that your brain sends you about your physical needs. You get a "hunger" signal, you do something . . . you eat. You get a "cold" signal, you do something . . . you put on extra clothes or turn up the thermostat.

It is much easier to recognize the urgent survival signals related to your physical needs than it is to recognize the painful internal signals related to your mental needs. You tend to simply dismiss these signals as not being important. Many times you dismiss them because when you think about them you simply don't know what to do. You say, "I'm angry," or "I'm depressed," or "I'm scared." But you don't DO or THINK anything to make yourself less angry, depressed, or scared. You try to ignore the signal and hope it will go away.

The truth is that the painful negative signal will not go away because it is telling you that you do not have enough love, power, fun, or freedom in your life. Sometimes you may think you have what you want, or what other people THINK you SHOULD want, and you still are getting negative signals. This is because if you examine what YOU REALLY WANT it may not be what you have in your life, even though you may "look" successful to others, or maybe even to yourself.

33

For example, having a high-powered job may be exactly right for someone else, but being a full-time mother is exactly right for you. Some people turn to drugs (alcohol, cocaine, etc.) when they get a painful negative signal that they don't want to recognize. Drugs act swiftly to get rid of the signal. But the problem is when the drugs wear off, the signal is still there, leading to – you guessed it – more drugs.

YOUR PAINFUL FEELINGS ARE CLUES

One of the best strategies you can use to get in touch with your negative signals is to start thinking of your painful feelings – both emotional and physical – as clues that are telling you that you are not getting what you want in life. Once you begin to recognize that these feelings are related to your signals, you can start thinking about what you want that you are not getting. Then you can do something to start getting what you want.

FOR EXAMPLE

Jake was a junior in high school when he began to be depressed frequently and to have headaches. He kept saying he didn't know what was the matter. I explained negative signals to him and asked him directly what he wanted that he wasn't getting. He said, "I don't know, things are OK." I said, "If your life were truly OK, you wouldn't be depressed and have headaches." Finally, he said, "I don't think my grades are going to be good enough to get into the college my father went to." Jake finally got up the nerve to talk to his father. To his surprise, his father said, "As long as you are trying hard, I'm happy wherever you go to college." Jake is now happier and his headaches have disappeared.

TRUST YOUR SIGNALS

Once you acknowledge the signal, you have to take the responsibility for doing something about getting what you need. Some people would rather believe that they have no control over their feelings than try to correct what is wrong. It's so easy to blame your feelings on other people.

One reason that psychosomatic illness is hard to cure is that people blame others: "She gave me a headache." Some people don't want to put any effort into getting what they really want. Others believe that no matter what they do, they won't get what they want. And some people don't think they should want anything. They choose to feel guilty. Figure out if you have any of these ideas and get rid of them if you want to be happier.

HOW CAN MY PERSONAL SURVIVAL ALARM SYSTEM HELP ME?

Knowing that you have internal signals – positive and negative, strong and weak – can help you get more of what you want in life. You have probably experienced an uneasy sensation and not recognized that it was an internal signal telling you something was wrong. Ignoring this uneasiness made things get worse, or even explode. For example, you are on your way to the airport and you have a moment of uneasiness. You recognize this internal signal, but do not try to figure out what is wrong. When you get to the ticket counter you discover that you have left your discounted ticket at home and you have to buy a new, full-fare ticket in order to make your flight.

On the other hand, you have probably gotten signals that told you things were going fine in your life and you ignored them too. For example, your entire family arrives safely at the beach for an enjoyable vacation. You never stop to think about how much each one of them means to you, and how glad you are that you didn't have a wreck on the way. In reality, most of the time things are not really pleasurable or really miserable. Your life, like most lives, is probably just so-so much of the time. It doesn't have to be that way. You can make the choice to be happier than you are now. Start by fine-tuning your ability to notice your own signals, the strong ones and the weak ones.

PART I
RECOGNIZING POSITIVE SIGNALS

Strong, happy people give themselves credit for what they have in their lives. They don't harp on themselves when they make mistakes. They don't whine about what they don't have.

They are able to recognize what they are doing right.

As simple as this sounds, a big difference between happy people and unhappy people is that happy people recognize when they are doing something to get what they want. The reason it is so difficult to notice when things are going right is that our brain is designed for survival: It sends us stronger signals when we are not getting what we want. In other words, there is no problem or danger when things are fine.

That's why it takes practice to notice your positive signals.

BEFORE YOU BEGIN,
THINK ABOUT THIS:

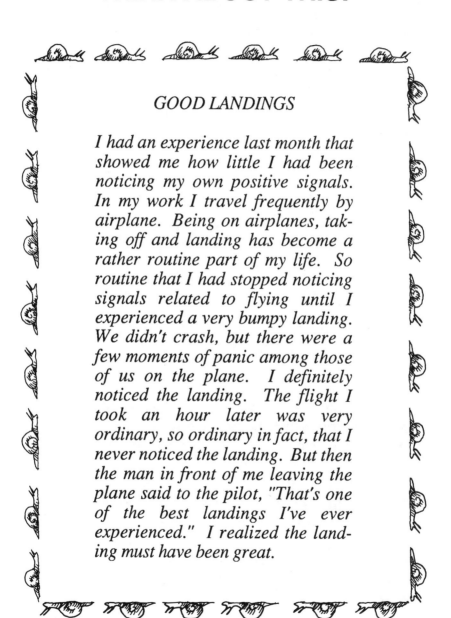

GOOD LANDINGS

I had an experience last month that showed me how little I had been noticing my own positive signals. In my work I travel frequently by airplane. Being on airplanes, taking off and landing has become a rather routine part of my life. So routine that I had stopped noticing signals related to flying until I experienced a very bumpy landing. We didn't crash, but there were a few moments of panic among those of us on the plane. I definitely noticed the landing. The flight I took an hour later was very ordinary, so ordinary in fact, that I never noticed the landing. But then the man in front of me leaving the plane said to the pilot, "That's one of the best landings I've ever experienced." I realized the landing must have been great.

I wondered at the time how many good landings I miss in my life because I take them for granted. There are probably lots of good happenings in life that you, like me, are not noticing. You may not be noticing the positive ways you are meeting your needs. You may not be giving yourself credit for what you are doing. You may be thinking about what you don't have instead of what you DO have. Are you recognizing the signals that are telling you the ways in which you are having good landings every day?

ARE PROBABLY HAPPIER THAN YOU THINK YOU ARE

because now you notice what's NOT right in your life much more than you notice what IS right. This helps you to survive, but it doesn't help you to be happy.

Learning to recognize when you are getting what you want is an essential part of being happy.

If you can recognize your positive signals, both strong and weak, you will be more satisfied with your life.

TARGET PRACTICE

NOTICING   POSITIVE   SIGNALS

In this target practice write down three times when you got what you wanted today. This is complicated because one of the ways you can recognize that you got what you wanted is to recognize that you didn't get what you didn't want. For example, I didn't get a bumpy landing or a plane crash. Therefore, to put it positively, I arrived at my destination with no hassles, which was exactly what I wanted.

When we are dealing with other people in our lives – spouses, parents, children, coworkers, bosses, professors – we are usually terrific at recognizing negative signals but lacking when it comes to recognizing positive ones. For example, most parents notice when their children are fighting. On the other hand, few parents notice when their children are having a calm evening. One of the reasons it is so hard to be happy is that we honestly don't pay much attention when we are getting our needs met. One key to being happy or satisfied with your life is to recognize when things are right, and give yourself credit for them.

 **I GOT WHAT I WANTED WHEN**

❶

❷

❸

Now, think about this a bit more. How did you know that you got what you wanted? Each person will get the signal a bit differently. It will also depend on how much you wanted what you got. For example, you will probably experience more intense signals if you desperately wanted to go to law school and got in, than if someone told you your sweater looked great.

In case you are stuck, here's a friend's list to give you an idea of how to start.

I GOT WHAT I WANTED WHEN

1 It was snowing this morning and the family was finally off. Instead of rushing as usual, I took the time to sit, have another cup of coffee and watch the snow. (I knew this was what I wanted when I had an immediate feeling of relaxation, followed by a calm body and mind. I thought about it and realized that I had met my need for freedom.)

2 A friend I hadn't seen in a week or so called and asked me to lunch. (I knew I got what I wanted when I felt a little rush of excitement. I thought about it and realized that I had met my need for belonging.)

3 My boss called me in to say that the clients I had worked with last week said I was terrific. (I knew I got what I wanted when I felt a zing in my chest. I thought about it and realized that I had met my need for power.)

As you look at your list, or my friend's, don't think these examples are unimportant. The more you recognize your signals telling you that you are meeting your needs, the happier you will be.

If you are having trouble recognizing POSITIVE signals, think about the last time you had your hair cut. Did you like the cut? Did it match your picture? If it did, you got a positive signal, you thought about it, and you said:

"This is it, this is how I want to look."

But – if the haircut wasn't what you wanted and you thought you looked terrible, you got a

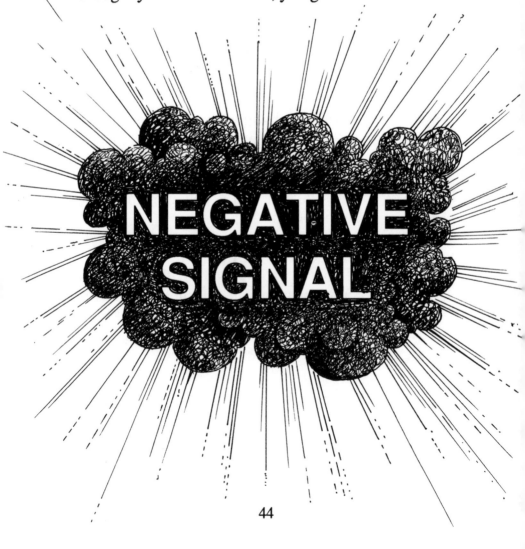

NEGATIVE SIGNAL

PART II
RECOGNIZING NEGATIVE SIGNALS

It's easier to recognize negative signals than positive ones. You will tend to notice negative signals more since they signal you that you are NOT getting something you want. Those negative signals that are the most difficult to notice – and the ones you MUST notice to be happier – have been "going off" for a long time.

SOME EXAMPLES

Tim says he has a sick feeling in the pit of his stomach each time his mother says, "When are you going to grow up? You're 40 and you don't have a real job yet."

Jackie says she feels her chest tightening when her boss takes credit for one of her ideas for the 20th time.

Your target is to STOP ignoring negative signals by recognizing them. This takes practice.

BEFORE YOU BEGIN, THINK ABOUT THIS

I parked my car downtown last week and was surprised by the very loud bell that rang each time a ticket left the slot of the parking gate. When I went back later to pick up my car, I asked the attendant how he could stand that loud bell going off right by his head, time after time. He looked puzzled by my question, then replied, "Oh, that, I don't even notice it anymore."

The same thing happens to many of your negative signals. They are so regular and such an accepted part of your life that you stop recognizing them. You begin to ignore the message that something is wrong.

The problem with this is that your brain isn't ignoring that something is wrong. If you don't consciously act to get what you want you may become sick, or depressed, or just feel miserable. You say that you don't know what's wrong.

Melody, a friend's daughter, was complaining of headaches at the beginning of the school year. Melody did not say that school was hard or stressful. My friend, concerned about the headaches, asked Melody when she got them. She said, "During English and math." Then she gave herself away. Melody said, "I never get them in spelling. Spelling is easy." By ignoring the negative signals coming her way in English and math and not acting to get rid of them, she began to get headaches. The signal is there, whether noticed or not.

YOUR SIGNALS, POSITIVE AND NEGATIVE, ARE RELENTLESS IN TRYING TO TELL YOU WHETHER YOU ARE MEETING YOUR NEEDS.

YOUR SIGNALS ARE TIED DIRECTLY TO THE PICTURES YOU HAVE OF HOW YOU WANT TO MEET YOUR NEEDS.

The easiest negative signals to recognize are those that are acute. You experience painful negative signals through your body and emotions. The signal is very brief: It lasts just long enough to give you the information you need. Instantly you know: pleasure... pain; it matches my picture ... it doesn't.

RECOGNIZE YOUR SIGNALS

When driving, have you ever had a near wreck, then continued down the road and noticed that your heart was racing, your palms were sweating and your feelings of fear were literally "in your throat?" If so, you have had a typical experience with very strong survival signals. The signals related to your mental needs can be just as acute, as anyone can understand who has experienced the loss of someone they loved.

Your negative signals are like alarm bells going off inside. Sometimes they sound like a four-alarm fire. Other times they are like a small beep. These signals are your brain's way of telling you that something is not the way you want it to be. These negative signals are messages that tell you whether you are getting what you need to be happy. And more important, they are telling you to do something.

A negative signal is the pure pain you automatically experience when you are confronted with an obvious problem. You probably believe that how you behave after the signal is also automatic. Not necessarily.

Your face may redden with anger when your mother-in-law insists on a visit. But if you later develop a headache, that's your way of intentionally acting on the bad news or negative signal.

You probably believe you can't help how you feel. That's half true. You can't choose the signal, but you can choose what you do after you get it. Did it ever occur to you that the headache you get before your mother-in-law's visit gives you an excuse not to talk to her?

Understand that you don't choose your signals but you choose what you do after you get a signal.

WHAT DO YOU CHOOSE

You CANNOT choose whether you will have internal signals telling you that what you really want is missing from your life. You cannot avoid wanting to survive.

That is the way your brain is designed.

If your needs aren't being met you will have PAIN – emotional or physical.

You CAN choose what to do when you get a painful signal. You can choose to ACT in a different way to get what you want. You can choose to THINK in a different way about what you want. But before you can act differently, or think differently, you have to recognize the negative signals you are receiving, be they soft or loud. You also have to understand the message they are giving you.

TARGET PRACTICE

Now it's time to practice recognizing your negative signals. First read the examples, then try it yourself. To give you a start, here is a list from another friend.

1 I wanted to wear my new blue suit to an important meeting and I remembered early this morning I had forgotten to pick it up at the tailor. (I knew it wasn't what I wanted when I felt instantly irritated, thought about it, and realized that I was angry because I wouldn't look my best at the meeting which wouldn't meet my need for power.)

2 I wanted my wife to meet me at the garage after work so I could leave the car to be tuned up, but she had a meeting. (I knew it wasn't what I wanted when I felt a flash of anger, thought about it, and realized that I want my wife to be available. I wasn't meeting my need for power and belonging.)

3 My son took the car without asking while I was out jogging and I had a tennis match and no way to get there. (I knew it wasn't what I wanted when I came around the corner and saw the car wasn't there. I had a hollow feeling in the pit of my stomach. I knew that I couldn't meet my need for fun and freedom.)

 **TAKE AIM**

Now it's your turn. In the space below, or on another sheet of paper, write down three times when you did not get what you wanted today. Try to include big wants and not-so-big wants.

I DID NOT GET WHAT I WANTED WHEN

Think a little more. How did you know that you did not get what you wanted? What do your negative signals feel like?

A BRIDGE

THE KEY TO RECOGNIZING
YOUR SIGNALS IS KNOWING
THEY ARE JUST THAT:
SIGNALS.

THEY ARE QUICK
AND ACUTE.

AFTER YOU RECOGNIZE THEM
YOU CAN CHOOSE TO IGNORE
THEM OR TO ACT ON THEM.

YOUR SIGNALS ARE TIED TO
YOUR PICTURES OF
WHAT YOU WANT TO MEET
YOUR NEEDS.

SEEING YOUR PICTURES
CLEARLY IS YOUR NEXT
TARGET.

PICTURES

❷ SEE YOUR PICTURES

THINK IT

You have mental pictures for each one of your basic needs.

These pictures are of what you want to meet your needs.

❶ One of your LOVE pictures may be receiving a dozen roses from someone who looks like Robert Redford and behaves like Alan Alda.

❷ One of your POWER pictures may be the words "Executive Vice President" written on your office door.

❸ One of your FUN pictures may be dancing all night with your love picture!

❹ And one of your FREEDOM pictures may involve snorkeling in the Caribbean.

Some of your pictures are developed and you have them in your life right now.

And some are still undeveloped.

In order to honestly meet your basic needs you have to notice the pictures you now have in your life and decide what others you want to add.

WANTS = PICTURES

WHERE DO MY PICTURES COME FROM?

As a newborn baby you had survival needs. The need for shelter, warmth and food. But you also had the same four needs we have been talking about:

LOVE
POWER
FUN
FREEDOM

As you acted and interacted in the world, you had experiences that met your needs.

For example, when you felt lonely, you probably cried or showed your discomfort in some way. Then a loving person in your family came to your crib, held you, talked to you, rocked you, or sang you a song. You got a positive internal signal. From these experiences you developed pictures of what love is. That is, your picture of love included being held, given attention, talked to, etc. When you experience a need being met you put the picture in your head. It becomes one of the ways you want to meet the need.

If you were not so lucky, and didn't have a loving person to come pick you up, you experienced the pain of not having your needs met from an early age.

Lucky or not, beginning when you were a baby and continuing throughout your life, you have collected pictures in your mind of how you want your needs met.

You now have a set of very specific, unique visual portraits of what you want to meet your needs.

Some of your pictures come from your experiences. Some of your pictures come from your culture. Some come from TV. Many come from advertising. In fact, advertisers know what you need and they systematically tie their products to your basic needs. For example, most people know that you can't smell Charlie perfume over the odors in a fancy restaurant, yet the heads of all the men in the restaurant turn as the model comes in wearing CHARLIE! Her need for power is met in an instant, all because she's wearing Charlie perfume. You are quickly reminded that Charlie can do the same for you. Many advertisers imply that you won't be sexually attractive if you don't use their product.

REMEMBER:

WE MEET OUR NEEDS THROUGH ACTIVITIES WE DO WITH OURSELVES AND OTHER PEOPLE – NOT THROUGH PRODUCTS.

You have very specific ideas about what you want for everything from dinner to romance. These pictures are your ideal world. They are what you would have in your life if it could be "ideal." They are not what you NEED. Your needs can still be satisfied, even if you don't get what you want. Remember the Rolling Stone's song:

You can't always get what you want,
but if you try sometime, you just might find, you
get what you need.

A HOLIDAY STORY

A prime time to see your pictures in action is during a specific holiday celebration. Most of us have definite holiday pictures. My friend Judith has a German mother-in-law, and Judith has had a hard time getting used to their differing Christmas pictures. Judith's Christmas picture includes lots of gifts, with expensive treasures being reserved for special relatives. To go along with those presents Judith pictures a large, ornate tree that must touch the ceiling. Imagine her surprise when she first saw her mother-in-law's "Christmas" home with a small tree adorned with a few handmade snowflakes and one gift for each person under the tree. Judith was embarrassed by her armload of flashy gifts (at least three for each person) but annoyed that she could not find her picture of Christmas anywhere. She experienced a negative signal as she looked around.

58

Holiday blues and Christmas conflicts can come from people's differing pictures, their search for the "right" picture, or the attitude that their picture is right and someone else's is wrong.

You can be a lot happier if you talk well in advance of the holidays about everyone's pictures. The only way to have a Christmas that is acceptable to all is to compromise and negotiate. It sounds like this: "OK, we can have goose instead of ham if we can have sweet potatoes instead of rice. Christmas is not Christmas without sweet potatoes." OR "It's important to me that I decorate the tree with the children, so we will come to your house two days before Christmas if you will wait and let us help pick out the tree and decorate it. We will even bring some of our special decorations. Is that all right with you?"

These examples may seem trivial, but many holidays could be happier if people figured out which "pictures" were truly important to them and which ones weren't. This kind of planning results in positive signals.

CAUTION:
YOUR PICTURES MAY BE HARMFUL TO YOUR HEALTH AND HAPPINESS

One large problem with your pictures is that they don't come labeled by the surgeon general as to whether they will help you meet your needs in the long run or even in the short run. This idea is very understandable in terms of food. Everyone knows that a candy bar is not as good for you as an apple. A candy bar tastes great at the moment you are eating it, but it has little nutritional value. On the other hand, life would be very dull with no candy bars. The trick is to both develop pictures that will meet your needs in the short run AND in the long run. Place some emphasis on those that will meet your needs in the long run. In other words, eat more apples than candy bars and you will probably be fine.

60

WHY DOES IT MATTER IF I KNOW WHAT MY PICTURES ARE?

In order to get what you want, in order to feel a sense of well-being or happiness in your life, you have to know what you want ideally. This doesn't mean you will always get everything you want, because, don't forget, everyone has pictures of what they want. Since we meet our needs through ourselves and OTHERS, we can't always get all of what we want. BUT, and this is a big but, the more you think about exactly what you want, the more likely you are to get it. If you can tell others what you want, and encourage them to tell you what they want, both of you have a good chance of getting most of what you want.

Often when we complain to those we are close to, we tell them what we DON'T want, not what we DO want.

WHY DO I SOMETIMES PRETEND I DON'T KNOW WHAT I WANT?

It's a big risk to tell yourself, much less someone else, what you want. It is really the essence of you. If someone laughs at what you want, or tells you that you don't have a chance of getting it, you get a negative signal. This signal is very painful because it tells you that you are not getting or going to get what you truly need. Also, when you admit what it is you really want, then you have the responsibility of making it happen. You have to act to get what you want.

PART I:
NOTICING WHAT YOU HAVE

Noticing what you have is like noticing your positive signals – you probably don't do it often enough. You focus more on what hurts, disappoints or angers you. More energy is put into trying to change your faults than in noticing your own strengths. In fact, you may, like many people, ignore your strengths to the extent that you are never truly satisfied with yourself. You never notice what you have done or are doing in your life that is right for you. Instead, you put increasing pressure on yourself to be a super person. Or, you may have just given up on yourself.

YOU ARE PROBABLY DOING A LOT BETTER THAN YOU THINK.

Since your brain is designed for survival, you notice more what you DON'T have than what you DO have. For example, many single parents forget what they do have, and forget to remind themselves of how great they are doing, usually under very difficult circumstances.

Another reason you don't give yourself credit for what is right in your life is that you, like most people, probably find it hard to equate what YOU DO with your own happiness. You probably believe that happiness has to do mostly with people and things outside yourself. You might say, "He makes me so happy" or "She makes me feel good." If you say this you don't understand that the good feelings come from within yourself. They come from the choice you make to develop strong relationships. That is something you have done.

TARGET PRACTICE

Take time right now to notice the parts of your life that meet your needs. Where do you feel good? What do you like about your life? (Be sure YOU think it's positive, not your mother, husband, wife, teacher or boss.)

Think about this from two points of view: First, what are you doing or what do you have from yourself that you like?

Then, what are you getting from other people that makes your life better?

WHAT I HAVE THAT MAKES MY LIFE HAPPIER

Example:

From myself:
1. a job
2. a home
3. parenting
4. jogging
5. reading
6. cooking

Your list:

From myself:

From others:

From others:

1. a family that cares
   about me (husband,
   daughter, mother)
2. interesting friends
   (they do lots of things
   I enjoy hearing about)
3. people to work with
   who are smart and care
4. people who tell me I help
   them and their programs

Next, give yourself credit for what you have done
in the past that has helped you. Think of things that
you have done that you believe you did right.
Then, decide what each of those accomplishments
says about you. Write it down. Think of some
"big" things and some "little" things.

WHAT I HAVE DONE RIGHT

Example:
At the age of 35 I decid-
ed I needed exercise and
started jogging. Now at
43 I jog 2-3 miles every
day.

Your turn:

WHAT THAT SAYS ABOUT ME

I have some discipline
and I am conscious of
my health.

DECIDE WHAT
YOU WANT

PART II:
DECIDING WHAT YOU WANT

Deciding what YOU honestly want to meet your basic needs is essential if you want to be happy. You now understand your personal survival alarm system. You now know that you have positive and negative signals which are related to what you want. After you recognize these signals you know to do one of two things:

1. **Positive Signals:**

Give yourself credit for getting what you wanted.

2. **Negative Signals:**

Figure out what you wanted that you didn't get.

THEN

Decide if you can try another way or ways to get it.

OR

Decide if another want could meet the same need.

TAKE AIM

Take a look at what you want to meet your needs that you don't have in your life right now. It could be as simple as some new clothes or as complex as a new career. Many times when you can't get one thing you want, you give up on meeting your needs because you don't have an ACTIVE WANT FILE.

You probably have an inactive want file. And you probably have a "maybe some day when the kids are grown" want file. And you probably have a "secret wish" want file.

When you are trying to decide if another want or picture could meet your needs bring out ALL of these files and CONSIDER them.

SAY WHAT YOU WANT

A picture is worth a thousand words.

Take a little time now, when you aren't experiencing a negative signal, to see what you want in your life that you don't have now. Use your unused files. Make a wish list of wants. Write down as many as you can in the space below.

MY WANTS:

Ask yourself the following questions about your list:

1. Can I get any of these things fairly easily?

2. If the "want" seems difficult to get, can I change the form of the want to make it more attainable?

FOR EXAMPLE: I want a new house but we can't afford one. What we need is more space so another want I could have is to add a room to the house we have.

3. When I get this, is it something that will really make me happy? (In the core of our being, if we ask ourselves hard questions, we KNOW when something will honestly make us happy.)

FOR EXAMPLE: Sometimes I think I want a job where I have my own coffee cup instead of the job I have now in which I travel frequently and am rarely in the same place twice. BUT, when I think honestly about this, I know that I am very happy doing what I do.

4. Will what I want make me happy in the long run or in the short run? (Remember apples and candy bars!) Even if we have a picture of something meeting our needs, if we honestly examine the want, we know that it WILL NOT, in the long run, get us what we want.

FOR EXAMPLE: A student might say, "I don't want to study for my big math test today because there is an all day party at the lake which will be fun." But if she fails out of school she won't get what she wants in the long run.

5. Is the price of what I want too high to pay?

FOR EXAMPLE: A friend once said to me, "I am very attracted to a co-worker who wants to have an affair with me. It would meet ALL of my needs now, but I love my husband and want to stay married. What if he found out?" The price was too high for her to pay; it wasn't worth it.

NEXT. . . have some fun thinking about what you want. Pretend a genie just came in and said you can have anything you want. BE CREATIVE. This time, put down everything, whether you think it's possible or not. GO WILD!!!!!!!!

WHAT DO YOU REALLY WANT?

When you finish, decide which of your basic needs each want would meet. Put L for love or belonging, P for power, F for fun and FR for freedom.

If the want would meet ALL of your needs then put a big ★. (If it meets two or three, put the code for the needs it would meet.)

Now you have two lists. My guess is that you know it is not possible to get all of what you want. Don't give up your dreams, but have an honest talk with yourself and decide what is possible in your life, what you are willing to pay for and what is not within your grasp. To give you an idea of what I mean, I want to tell a story about my little dachshund, Topsy.

CHASING HELICOPTERS
(A real life fable)

Topsy loves to go to the beach. She plays with the children and chases waves until she is worn out. Last summer she thought she had found some new toys when a military base began having "operations" over our beach. Topsy's new toys were the army helicopters. As they went by, Topsy would run furiously down the beach, jumping and trying to catch one. Of course, each time her short legs would fail and she would trot back to our blanket. Each time she chased a helicopter, however, she ran a shorter distance down the beach. When the fifth one flew by, Topsy just lifted her head and watched. She then put her head on the blanket with a sigh.

71

You probably have some helicopters you have been chasing. They might have looked ideal, and exactly like what you wanted when you started. If you have wanted something for a long time (my guess is about five years, but you know in your heart what is a long time for you) and you haven't gotten it, it may be a HELICOPTER for you. You don't have to give up wanting what you want, but there are ways of making your life happier WITHOUT that particular want.

First, figure out what NEED would be met by what you want but haven't been able to get.

Second, decide what you could substitute to meet the same need. (For Topsy, it was a Frisbee. I bought her one the next day and she became a terrific Frisbee catcher.)

REMEMBER:

You don't have to give up what you want, but while you are waiting to "get it" you can add other wants that will meet the same need or needs.

In the space below, list one thing you could add to your life.

SOMETHING I COULD ADD TO MY LIFE:

IT WOULD MEET MY NEED(S) FOR:

BEHAVIORS

❸ CHOOSE YOUR BEHAVIORS

You have a powerful system which is designed to help you meet your needs.

It is there to help you get what you want.

It is called your BEHAVIORAL SYSTEM.

Sometimes you are conscious of it. Other times you are not. BUT, whether or not you are aware of it, it is working all the time.

**YOUR BEHAVIORAL SYSTEM
IS WORKING ALL THE TIME.**

**IT IS TRYING TO GET
YOU WHAT YOU WANT.**

**IF YOU UNDERSTAND IT, YOU
CAN MAKE IT WORK FOR YOU.**

WHAT ARE THE PARTS OF MY BEHAVIORAL SYSTEM?

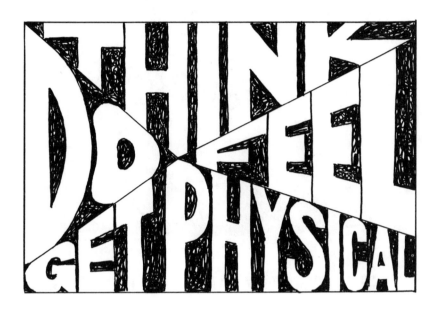

Your behavioral system is composed of four inter-locking parts. They operate together every time you behave. When you behave you DO, THINK, FEEL and GET PHYSICAL. For example, let's say you are changing a flat tire. That's what you are DOING. At the same time you are THINKING that you will be late for an important meeting. You are also FEELING angry that it happened to you. And finally, you GET PHYSICAL and are exhausted.

**ALL FOUR PARTS ARE INVOLVED
EVERY TIME YOU BEHAVE.**

When you say, "I feel depressed," you probably don't think about what you are doing, what you are thinking, and what your body is telling you. But whether or not you are thinking about it, the other three parts of the system are there.

WHAT EXACTLY ARE MY FEELINGS?

Most of us have been "trained" to believe that our feelings are sacred and definitely something over which we have no control. This is partially true. You do not have control over your signals (which you experience as physical sensations), and you do not have control over the feelings that are a part of what you are thinking and doing. BEHAVIOR IS TOTAL. What you DO have control over is what you think and do after you get a signal. Often when you get a negative signal you think, "This is not what I want," and how you continue to think about it will bring with it anger (they're doing it to me again), depression (I'm never going to get what I want), annoyance (why doesn't she leave me alone?) or fear (what if he finds out?).

You probably do not believe that the words "feeling" and "behavior" go together. You do not think of your feelings as part of your behavioral system. Knowing that your thoughts and actions have a feeling component is POWERFUL INFORMATION. How you are feeling depends on what you are doing and thinking. It's up to you. If you are using your thoughts and actions to get what you need, you have a good chance of experiencing a feeling of happiness or satisfaction.

DO I REALLY CHOOSE MY BEHAVIORS?

It is hard to believe that you CHOOSE your behaviors. It is especially hard to believe that you choose behaviors which do not make you happy. But you do. I do, we all do. You probably don't believe you have as much control over your behaviors as you in fact do have. You can always behave in another way. You can make the choice in a few seconds.

The problem is that our behaviors are habits. So, we might WANT to choose another behavior but keep going back to our old, "bad habit" behavior. There are ways to get around this if you take it nice and easy and don't expect to change over night. **GO SLOWLY.**

Mark Twain said that to get rid of a bad habit, you couldn't throw it out the window, you had to coax it down the stairs, one step at a time. The same is true of your behaviors.

JACOB

I have a good friend who thought negatively about himself literally ALL THE TIME. When I realized how often he used ineffective thinking behaviors I asked him if he thought it was helping him to be happy to think about himself in negative ways day in and day out. He said, "NO." He then began to counter each negative thought with a positive one. "I will never find a job I like" was changed to "I have had four jobs I liked very much in the past 10 years. I did them very well and I WILL find another one." He began by doing this exercise on audio tape. He started by working on five negative thoughts a day. He slowly began to change his ineffective thinking behaviors to effective thinking behaviors. He still has to work hard at this, but slowly he is changing. He is happier about himself.

WHAT TRIGGERS MY BEHAVIORAL SYSTEM?

Remember your personal survival alarm system? These internal SIGNALS trigger your behavioral system. This is why it is so important for you to begin to recognize your signals.

You have NO CONTROL over your signals. You experience them as physical sensations and

INSTANTLY

whether or not you recognize your signals, you start behaving to get what you want.

So, when your powerful behavioral system gets the message that you aren't getting what you want, it goes to work. Or, YOU go to work. (Your behavioral system is YOU – without it, you would not be you!)

Often, when you start behaving – especially if you have gotten a painful, negative signal – you think, "This is not what I want." And you continue to think, "No matter how hard I try, I'll never get it." With this thought you experience the painful feeling component of your ineffective thinking behavior, perhaps depression.

If you don't choose to act or think differently, the painful feelings will probably increase.

83

ARE ALL MY BEHAVIORS EFFECTIVE?

NO

But all of your behaviors are trying to get you what you want. You are always doing THE BEST YOU CAN to meet your needs.

Obviously, some of your behaviors are more effective than others. Some of your behaviors are just plain ineffective. Ineffective behaviors make a bad situation worse – like watching TV when you have a term paper due in two days.

Some of your behaviors are like band-aids. They may help in the short run but don't help in the long run. They sometimes cover up the fact that you aren't getting what you want. They give you the ILLUSION you are getting what you need. You may feel better temporarily. You may use them to try to meet your needs at the expense of another person. You'll notice that with many of your band-aid behaviors you are trying to control the people around you through what you say to them or do to them or how you express your feelings to them. You are trying to get them to do what you want them to do. A wife might persuade her husband to turn down a promotion by saying, "If you really love me you won't take a job in another town. I like it here." That approach might meet her needs, but would her husband meet his? In the long run, her husband would probably resent her. The behavior she chose is a band-aid behavior.

EFFECTIVE BEHAVIORS

are those that will get you what you want in the long run, like a good relationship with your spouse, parent or child. Your effective behaviors will get you what you want without preventing the people around you from meeting their needs. For example, the wife might have compromised with her husband by saying,

"I know that you can't help it that the promotion is in another town, and even though I don't want to move, it would make it a lot better for me if I knew that I could go to graduate school since there is an excellent one there. If we move, will you support my effort to go back to school by assuming some of the housework?"

This is an effective behavior because it makes the relationship with her husband better, and both people get some of what they want.

It's smart to take a close look at your ineffective and band-aid behaviors if you want to be happy with yourself. You won't always avoid ineffective and band-aid behaviors, but try to use your effective behaviors most of the time.

THINK ABOUT THIS

The only person who knows whether your behaviors are effective to meet your basic needs,
LOVE, POWER, FUN AND FREEDOM,
IS

YOU.

WHICH BEHAVIORS CAN I CHANGE EASILY?

The easiest behaviors to change are your DOING and THINKING behaviors. You have control over them while you do not have DIRECT control over your feeling and your physical behaviors. However, if you change what you are DOING you will change how you are FEELING. (Remember that all four parts work together.)

You probably already know this, if you think about it. Have you ever been depressed and a friend called and asked you to go out? Even though you didn't really feel like going out, you went anyway and had an interesting conversation with your friend. You were surprised halfway through dinner to realize that you weren't so depressed anymore. But most of the time when you are depressed you don't want to do anything. Except stay at home and be depressed.

SOMETHING TO THINK ABOUT OR, HOW TO FEEL BETTER FASTER

If you are depressed and you change what you are doing and thinking, you should feel somewhat better. However, sometimes you change what you are doing and thinking and you still feel lousy.

What you are DOING has NOTHING to do with what your SIGNAL was about.

IF YOU THINK ABOUT WHAT YOU WANTED THAT YOU DIDN'T GET AND START TO DO SOMETHING TO GET IT, YOU WILL FEEL BETTER INSTANTLY.

If, however, you don't pay much attention to the signal and you start doing something different, you will probably feel somewhat better, but not as GOOD as you could feel if you started DOING something to get what you really want.

THIS TAKES PRACTICE!

AN EXAMPLE:

A friend tells you that she heard in the neighborhood that it is your teenager who is leading the beer parties in the woods. You get an INTERNAL SIGNAL, think about it, and realize that your picture of being a good mother does NOT include your teenager in the woods drinking beer. YOU start DOING something. What you choose to do is to exercise. You run for half an hour.

DO YOU FEEL BETTER? YES!

BUT do you feel as good as you could feel if you had started to DO something about the problem related to the signal? NO!

What if, instead of exercising, you had gone to the junior high and asked your daughter if she had been drinking beer. She said yes. You restricted her freedom or privileges and talked to her about what she could do instead of drink beer when she wanted some fun and freedom.

OR

If you had gone to the junior high and talked to your daughter who promised it wasn't she, and then you had called your neighbor, you would have felt better faster.

Neither action made the situation perfect, but YOU felt better because you got more of your picture of yourself as a good mother.

WHAT YOU CHOSE TO DO FITTED WITH WHAT YOU WANTED.

PART I:
RECOGNIZING INEFFECTIVE, BAND-AID AND EFFECTIVE BEHAVIORS

It's helpful to start learning to recognize the behaviors you and those around you are using to meet your needs with people or situations in your lives.

There are 3 kinds of behaviors you are using:

① INEFFECTIVE: Make a bad situation worse and you don't feel any better.

② BAND-AID: May help for the moment, but not in the long run. You temporarily feel better.

③ EFFECTIVE: Get you what you need in the long run without preventing others from meeting their needs.

INEFFECTIVE BEHAVIORS

Some of your behaviors are just INEFFECTIVE and usually make a bad situation worse. When you use them you don't feel better, you may even feel worse. For example, when you're depressed about not having enough money you may quit the job you have, and then have no money.

BAND-AID BEHAVIORS

Your BAND-AID behaviors offer short-term solutions to your problems. You might blame your shortage of money on your children and yell at them. This band-aid behavior may make you feel better for a while, but the problem of not enough money is no closer to being solved. Sometimes you may use a band-aid behavior to deal with a person or situation without realizing you are doing it. For example, going out for drinks after work every night may be easier than talking to your wife about your unhappiness with your marriage.

EFFECTIVE BEHAVIORS

EFFECTIVE behaviors are those which in the long run will get you what you want without causing harm to yourself or those around you. Asking your boss for a small raise, looking for a higher paying job, or getting a part-time job are all effective behaviors to use when you don't have enough money.

# TARGET PRACTICE

In this section you'll work on becoming more aware of exactly which behaviors are ineffective, which are band-aid behaviors, and which are effective behaviors in some fairly typical situations.

Read the examples and see if you recognize any of the behaviors you use daily. If you can think of any behaviors you use, or you have seen others use in the same situation (or a similiar one) add them to the list. The following examples include doing, thinking and feeling. There is also a physical component to these behaviors which you will think about in the next section.

SITUATION ONE:
I'M UNHAPPY IN MY MARRIAGE:

INEFFECTIVE

- Be depressed.
- Don't talk to spouse.
- Leave without trying.
- Criticize spouse.
- Say I'm unlovable.
- Nag.

BAND-AID

- Be unfaithful.
- Stay with friends.
- Drink a lot.
- Work excessively.
- Come home rarely.

EFFECTIVE

THINK:
What do I want?
- DO: Tell spouse what you've discovered without criticism.
- Plan a fun evening doing what you used to enjoy together.

94

SITUATION TWO:
MY CHILD ISN'T DOING WELL
IN SCHOOL

INEFFECTIVE	BAND-AID	EFFECTIVE
• Tell child he's a failure. • Tell yourself you are not a good mother. • Criticize the child. • Nag. • Spank him.	• Threaten him until he does his homework. • Tell him you are disappointed in him and he has to do better. • Compare him to his sister who makes A's.	• THINK: He can improve. I can help. • Maybe I expect too much. • DO: Talk to his teacher. • Tell him you care. • Help him. • Find a tutor.

SITUATION THREE:
I WASN'T INVITED TO THE BIG PARTY
AT JOHN'S HOUSE

INEFFECTIVE	BAND-AID	EFFECTIVE
• Tell yourself you are ugly. • Tell yourself you are unlikeable. • Be depressed.	• Get high. • Start a nasty rumor about John. • Fight with your little sister. • Complain to your mother.	THINK: It's a party not my whole life. There must be someone else who's not invited. • DO: Ask a friend out. • Ask John to play tennis. • Go look at colleges that weekend.

 **TAKE AIM**

YOUR TURN: Think of a situation for yourself that you are having a problem with:

_____

Ask yourself these questions and fill in the chart below: What are the ineffective behaviors I am currently using? Many ineffective behaviors involve criticizing yourself or others.

What are the band-aid behaviors I am currently using? Many band-aid behaviors involve rationalizing the situation so it doesn't seem so bad.

What are the effective behaviors I am currently using and what other effective behaviors could I use? To find more effective behaviors:

THINK: What do I need that I'm not getting?
What do I really want in this situation?
What can I do differently than I am doing?

DO: Compromise. Find help. Ask for it. Get more information. Negotiate. Take action.

INEFFECTIVE   BAND-AID   EFFECTIVE

SOON AFTER I FOUND OUT, I BROKE OUT IN HIVES ALL OVER MY BODY.

PART II:
RECOGNIZING WHAT YOUR BODY IS TELLING YOU

Your behavior is total, so every time you behave you "get physical." You may view physical pain or illness as something that just happens. Sometimes this is true. But many times your physical condition is a part of the total behavior that you are using to meet your needs.

Your body is a kind of barometer that tells you how you are meeting your needs.

Have you heard someone say, "Soon after I found out that I didn't get the job, I broke out in hives all over my body." Or, "Six months after Don died, I found out I had cancer." Or, "After I found out I couldn't get pregnant, I started having migraine headaches." These are the physical components of doing and thinking behaviors.

The following scale is a list to assist you in assessing the physical component of the behaviors you are using in your life.

Rate yourself on the barometer below. Which number describes you best? Be honest.

THE BODY BAROMETER

1 I have physical pain much of the time which prevents me from doing what I want to do.

2 I periodically experience physical pain located in one area of my body or a disease for which the doctors cannot find a physical cause.

3 I have a variety of physical ailments. I never know what's going next. I am sick a lot.

4 I am not ill, but in poor physical shape.

5 I am tired much of the time; I only do what I HAVE to do.

6 I am average in health, with the normal amount of sick days.

7 Sometimes I am tired or tense but I know what actions to take to get back to normal.

8 I am seldom physically ill.

9 I use strength-building and tension-releasing techniques regularly such as jogging, meditating, martial arts, etc. I am hardly ever sick.

10 I am in excellent physical condition for my age and stay in good health.

If you have rated yourself 1 to 5 on the barometer, take a serious look at what you want, what you need, and the behaviors that you are using to meet your needs now. If you change what you are doing and thinking and start using more effective behaviors to meet your needs, you may find that your body is doing better, too.

IT WON'T HURT, AND IT MIGHT HELP.

NEEDS

❹ BALANCE YOUR NEEDS

To get what you want, you must know how to balance your needs.

If you are meeting one need but not the others you will be unhappy; you will know that something is missing in your life.

The best way to balance your needs is to

- be involved with enough different people so you can meet ALL your needs and

- do enough different activities to meet ALL your needs

THINKING about whether your needs are balanced is the first step toward balance. The second step is DOING SOMETHING about it.

TAKE ACTION to help yourself and the people in your life learn to meet each other's needs.

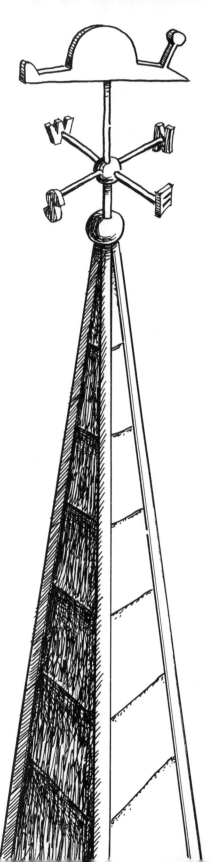

BALANCING

is easier to talk about than to do. If you have ever walked on a balance beam or on a log across a rushing brook, you know what I mean. A key to being happier with your life is learning to balance your needs. In other words, if you have LOTS of LOVE but no POWER you will not be happy. You will know something is missing in your life but you may not be sure what it is.

YOUR BODY AND MIND WORK FOR YOU IF YOU HELP

It is important to know how your system works to get you what you want. You have two systems working for you: a physical system and a mental system. These systems are linked; obviously they are both in the same body, but think about them separately for a moment.

102

YOUR BODY NEEDS BALANCE

An important element maintaining your physical system is balance. To have your body in perfect condition you have to balance diet, exercise and rest. Your body instinctively knows this. Contrary to what you might think, studies have shown that young children will not eat sweets all day long if left alone. Instead, given a choice of foods, they will naturally balance their diets.

Adult learning often ruins these skills. Do you balance what you eat each day? Do you frequently overindulge with rich food and drink, then try to compensate by dieting or fasting? That's not balance and it's not what your body needs. You might also exercise TOO much. It's not uncommon these days.

YOUR MIND NEEDS BALANCE

Your mind must also be balanced. This means that the way you meet your mental needs must be balanced. You cannot, for example, have a lot of love and belonging and no power, and still be happy. This explains why many teenagers who have parents who truly care about them still are not happy if they are not doing well in school. School is the main place kids have to meet their need for power, and many of them are not able to do so in our present school structure.

Overindulging one need, or denying yourself opportunities to meet another, will not lead to feeling good about yourself, or, to put it another way, to mental strength.

Here are some examples of people who were meeting some of their needs but had no BALANCE and consequently were unhappy with their lives.

ELAINE

Elaine devotes herself to home life.

As wife and mother of three, she has decided to manage her home full time. Consequently, she assumes responsibility for running the house, supporting her husband's career, managing the family bookkeeping and organizing the family's social life. She accomplishes these responsiblities efficiently and feels loving as she does her work each day. She finds time to make homemade bread, desserts and elegant dinners for the family and for guests; and to volunteer at her son's school. The activities and the commitments leave her feeling warm since her family and friends appreciate her efforts and say so with words and hugs.

She feels successful and appreciated and has a satisfying sense of belonging with other people. Her volunteer work touches many people's lives and Elaine feels important when she thinks about herself and this work. Yet Elaine does not feel happy.

What is wrong? She questions herself privately and often. She has no money worries since her husband earns a good living, and she does not worry because she doesn't have a salaried job or income-producing work.

But, Elaine discovers she doesn't ever do anything that is free of responsibility to someone else. She doesn't have just plain fun. It never occurred to Elaine before that she doesn't do much just for herself. She didn't realize that was important for her happiness to have a sense of freedom from time and responsibility and to have some fun in her life.

There is a strong sense of belonging and some power but little fun and freedom. A fairly typical pattern for a person who takes care of a family and a home.

ROBERT

Robert is the envy of his friends – especially of his married friends. He is handsome, single, wealthy, and successful. Every weekend includes an adventure, new places, new people. Robert isn't shallow, mind you; he thoroughly enjoys his friends and the places he goes. His charm, genuine friendliness and wit draw many people. And the four women he dates are pleased to spend time with him. At 32, he has what would be called a fine life.

And he is creative as well as generous. At Christmas time he personally selects and wraps gifts for each of his employees. He doesn't seem to mind that gifts from his employees are less personal, some cologne and a clothes brush to name a few.

He does mind, though, that too many times he feels empty. Something is missing, he says, but he can't figure out what it is.

With some help, he understands that each person has a need for love and belonging, for a deeply rooted connection to another person and cooperation with other people. He has been so busy, his life has been so full and so rushed, he hasn't developed any relationships based on commitments – those in which one feels "I'll be there for you in good times and bad."

Without love and belonging, Robert can't feel happy, even though the rest of his life is full.

There is fun, freedom and power but not much love and belonging.

KEVIN

In high school Kevin had been very smart. And though his family couldn't pay any tuition, he had made up his mind to go to the university. Strong support from high school teachers and subsequent scholarships helped him on his way. Finally he is there, a college student, his dreams come true.

He takes six classes which require being in class from 8 a.m. until 3 p.m. every day and he attends two evening labs. After classes he studies for two hours and works out until 11 or 12 each night. On weekends he does errands and laundry or catches up on papers, test preparations and projects.

He is making good grades but he is miserable. Why, he asks himself, am I so unhappy when I have everything I want?

Kevin figures out that he is feeling powerful as a student and has kept physically fit, but that the "A" transcript and the "A" muscular build don't meet his needs for fun, freedom and belonging with other people.

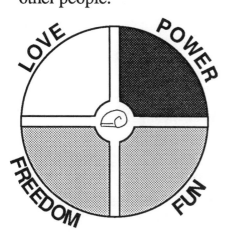

There is plenty of power but not much love, fun or freedom.

EACH OF THESE PEOPLE HAD OTHER PEOPLE AND ACTIVITIES IN THEIR LIVES, BUT THEY DID NOT HAVE

BALANCE

PART I:
BALANCING YOUR NEEDS

You can get more of what you want in your life if you learn the fine art of balancing. Please note: Juggling is NOT the same as balancing. When you have balance in your life, you have equality in the way that you meet your needs. You have an inner sense of calm. You feel centered. When you are juggling you are frantic, fearing that at any moment you will "drop the ball."

If you try to meet your basic needs by juggling people and activities you will never be happy.

TARGET PRACTICE

NOW

Consider the issue of balance in your activities and relationships. In the Target Practice for Chapter 2 you listed ways in which you are now meeting your needs through yourself. (You also listed additional ways in which you would like to meet your needs.) In this section you will be using the list of how you are now meeting your needs.

On the following pages, you are going to analyze the ways in which the people and activities in your life meet your needs.

TO START

On the PEOPLE page, list the name of a significant person in your life and analyze how he or she meets your need for LOVE. Then analyze how that person meets your need for POWER, FUN, and FREEDOM. On separate pages, do this for each significant person in your life.

THEN

Turn now to the questions concerning your ACTIVITIES and ask yourself how each important activity contributes to your need for LOVE, POWER, FUN, FREEDOM. Use separate sheets of paper for each important activity.

This is not supposed to be easy. In fact, the first time I tried I couldn't even do this exercise. It was a lot harder than I thought it would be to answer the questions HONESTLY.

For example, I thought my daughter met all my needs, but when I considered this, I realized that she meets my need for LOVE, POWER, and FUN but NOT FREEDOM.

Children rarely meet a parent's need for freedom. What does that mean? Get rid of children? Of course not. It simply means that understanding this, I have to meet my need for freedom through other people (good friends who still like me, even if I don't call them for month) or activities that I do myself (jogging). The thing to remember is that I must have freedom to balance my needs.

QUESTIONS TO ASK
YOURSELF ABOUT PEOPLE

Name a significant person in your life

LOVE

Does this person meet my need for love
and belonging?
Does s/he love me no matter what?
(unconditional love)
Do I feel a true sense of belonging
and closeness?
Does s/he care about me and what
happens to me?
Is s/he there in good times and in bad times?

POWER

Does this person meet my need for power?
Does s/he respect my opinions?
Do I feel important when I am with him/her?
Does s/he respect my skills and competence?
Does s/he give me recognition, praise?

111

FUN

Does this person meet my need for fun?
Do we laugh together?
Do we play together?
Do we share good times?
Do we learn together?.
Do we make discoveries together?
Do we have adventures?

FREEDOM

Does this person meet my need for freedom?
Does s/he allow me to be independent?
Does s/he let me make my own decisions?
Do I feel free with this person?
Do I make some of the choices about what we do?

NOTE: If this person is not meeting your needs, you probably are not meeting theirs either.

QUESTIONS TO ASK
YOURSELF ABOUT ACTIVITIES

> Name an important activity

LOVE

When I do this, do I feel like I belong to a team, a group, a family, a club?

POWER

When I do this, do I feel important, skilled, competent, disciplined?

FUN

When I do this, do I feel pleasure, am I having fun, am I making discoveries, am I truly enjoying myself?

FREEDOM

When I do this, do I feel in charge of myself, independent, able to make choices and decisions?

YOUR CIRCLE

Now, make a circle for yourself, using the information from your PEOPLE and ACTIVITIES sheets. If a person or activity meets all of your needs put it in each quadrant. If you think the person or activity meets only one need, for example LOVE, put it in the love quadrant.

Here is my circle for you to use as a sample.

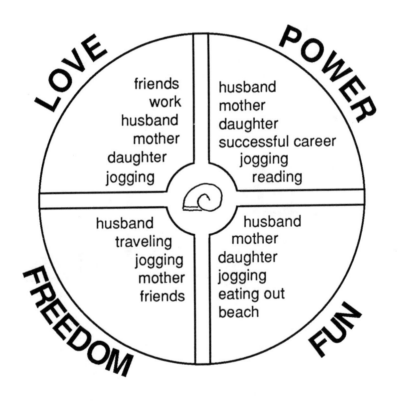

Now, it's your turn.

Look at your circle:

- Is it balanced? Is there a quadrant with not much in it?

- Do some quadrants list more than one person/activity? If so, terrific.

- Are there people and activities in your life meeting one need but not the others?

ACHIEVING A BALANCE

Look at your circle. Do you have people in your life who are each meeting one or two of your needs? Do you have activities that are only meeting one need? If so, you probably feel like you are juggling most of the time.

The way to get rid of juggling and to achieve balance is to work to have people and activities in your life that meet all of your needs. That would mean, for example, that with your spouse you had love, power, fun and freedom.

When you know something is missing in your life the tendency is to add something else instead of improving what you already have. Sometimes adding is perfect. Especially if what you add meets ALL your needs. Sometimes improving what you have is more need-fulfilling.

When I did my needs circle I discovered that my friend June gives me love and belonging but not much power, fun or freedom. I decided that this friendship was important to me. I set about to make our relationship more need-fulfilling. It worked. Now June is a person who meets all my needs. (And I meet hers.)

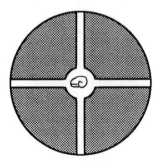

PART II:
MAINTENANCE

A part of life that can't be overlooked is maintenance. What would happen if you never took your car in for a tune-up or an oil change? Your relationships also need maintenance but are much less likely to get it. One reason for this is that we don't THINK about maintaining relationships. Consider how much time people spend planning weddings and how little time they spend figuring out how to maintain a good relationship after the ceremony.

It's equally important to maintain your activities – your job, hobby or recreational interests. If you don't maintain these important areas, they could disappear from your life. You could lose your touch.

IF YOU WANT TO BE HAPPY YOU HAVE TO MAINTAIN WHAT YOU HAVE.

Often, you get lazy when you get what you want. For example, when you lose five pounds you quit dieting and soon the weight is back. You frequently wait until something is broken beyond repair before you try to fix it. You do not pay attention to the warning lights in your life. A way out of this is to use your thinking behaviors to create maintenance signals for yourself to help you notice the warning lights.

When things are going OK in your relationships, you forget that you have to keep doing what you are doing to keep everything OK. Otherwise, relationships will fall apart or cease to be need-fulfilling.

This sounds simple,

but many marriages fall apart because couples forget they have to DO something to maintain the relationship.

There's a Victorian novel that opens with the husband coming down on the morning after the wedding and saying to his wife, "My dear, I love you now and I will always love you until I die. Let's not mention it again." Few wives today would be satisfied with this approach.

Most of us don't believe things can get worse – but if your relationships are not maintained, they can, and usually do, get worse.

THINGS COULD BE WORSE

If you look at the needs circle you just completed you will probably notice that there are people whom you haven't seen and activities that you haven't done for a while, even though you view them as important to you.

There might also be people in your needs circle whom you see often, but the quality of the relationship is not all you want it to be. You might have thought to yourself, "I'm not happy with this relationship."

TARGET PRACTICE

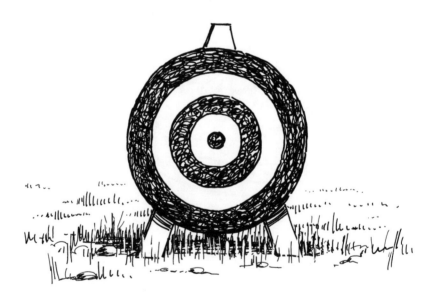

Go back to your needs circle and decide what actions you will take to maintain what you already have. Pick at least three items from your chart.

Examples: In order to continue having fun with my daughter, I will plan one outing for the two of us each Sunday.

In order to continue being the best at my job, sometime in the next three months I will attend a seminar on new advertising techniques.

In order to continue winning the recreation department tennis tournaments, I will practice tennis three times a week (unless it's snowing).

Your turn:

❶ In order to continue _____,

   I will _____.

❷ In order to continue _____,

   I will _____.

❸ In order to continue _____,

   I will _____.

It's up to you to maintain what you have while meeting your needs in a balanced way.

MAINTENANCE is a long-term behavior used by successful people. If you are not meeting your needs in a balanced way with long-term behaviors you are probably meeting them with ineffective, short-term behaviors.

OPTIONS

❺ INCREASE YOUR OPTIONS

Being happy requires variety as well as balance.

You will certainly be happier if your needs are in balance and you pay attention to meeting all four of your needs every day. But, just like eating the same meal every night for the rest of your life, if you don't ever change HOW you meet your needs, you will begin to get bored with your life.

You will realize that you could be doing and getting more out of life. You can get more out of life if you are willing to INCREASE YOUR OPTIONS for meeting your needs.

124

WHY BOTHER THINKING ABOUT VARIETY?

There are several good reasons to think about creating a varied needs circle.

REASON NUMBER ONE

It's hard to be happy if you expect too much from the wrong people or activities. For example, you may be spending time and energy on someone who is not really interested in your happiness, or on some activity that doesn't excite you at all. If that's true, try to eliminate those people or activities from your daily routine.

Okay, so maybe you are the only one who has the patience to deal with your selfish but sickly father-in-law, or who was generous enough to sign up for the local charity drive. All of us have commitments and responsibilities and no one is asking you to shirk those just for your own immediate gratification. But, make sure you are not drowning in unfulfilling tasks – that you find time for the people and activities that do excite you. Otherwise, you have only yourself to blame if you're not happy.

Now, think about the things you wished for in Chapter 2 on page 68. Then think about the people and activities in your life. What would happen if you spent less time with people who clearly do not meet or care to meet your needs? Or you gave up an activity that doesn't do anything for you?

Chances are, you'd have more time to spend getting some of the things on your wish list.

Face the reality that you do not have exactly the same friends or interests that you had five years ago. You may have become friends with someone simply because you both liked to play tennis. If your relationship revolves around weekly tennis matches that you no longer enjoy, maybe you should be spending less time with that friend. Or maybe you just need to admit you no longer enjoy tennis and see if you and your friend can enjoy doing some other activity together like really getting to know one another. It's always easier to continue a relationship or hobby that is no longer satisfying than to go out and find a new friend or interest.

But taking the easy path will probably not lead to your happiness.

THE HARSH REALITY:
You have to meet your needs every day.

THE HARSHER REALITY:
There are only 24 hours in the day.

THE HARSHEST REALITY:
If you spend time with people and on activities that don't fully meet your needs, you won't be happy.

REASON NUMBER TWO

Knowing that there are other pictures you can develop to meet your needs can give you a deep sense of security since life is never certain.

FACT:

ANY THING OR PERSON IN YOUR LIFE TODAY COULD NOT BE THERE TOMORROW.

Developing ways to meet your needs in the future can give you a sense of what you'll do when the people and activities on your chart NOW are no longer available to you. For whatever the reason. Think about the following possibilities:

- Your best friend tells you she's in love with your boyfriend, and he's in love with her.

- You've been jogging for the last 10 years and just broke your ankle.

- Your son, a junior in college, is hit by a car and has a severe brain injury.

- With no warning at all, your boss says the company has to cut back, and he is starting with you.

- Your wife says it's nothing personal, and she's not in love with anyone else, but she wants a divorce. You can have the kids.

- You are in a serious accident at work, and although your injuries don't prevent you from working, you are given an early retirement.

- Your only child has married and moved as far from you as she can live and still be in the country.

What would you do if a person who fulfills all or most of your needs lost interest or even died? It happens to all of us sooner or later. Think about how you would go about surviving and eventually becoming happy again. It's important to envision a variety of ways to meet your needs so that you'll always have an idea of how you can continue to find satisfaction in your life, no matter what. Think of this as

YOUR OWN PRIVATE EMERGENCY PLAN

REASON NUMBER THREE

The best possible psychological "diet" for you is one that is balanced and varied. The best psychological "food" meets more than one and, preferably, all of your needs. By developing a needs circle that has the same people and activities in each one of the need areas, you are maximizing how you meet your needs. If you add people and activities from your wish list you might find that some are more need-fulfilling than those you now have. You also might find that what you thought would be true is not.

BEWARE OF WHAT YOU WANT.

YOU JUST MIGHT GET IT!

SOMETHING TO THINK ABOUT

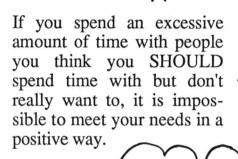

If you spend an excessive amount of time with people you think you SHOULD spend time with but don't really want to, it is impossible to meet your needs in a positive way.

If you spend an excessive amount of time using drugs of any kind it is impossible to meet your needs in a positive way.

If you watch an excessive amount of TV it is impossible to meet your needs in a positive way.

A very wise person once said:

Every choice you make, everything you do, is a kind of cage. It is a cage because by being this or choosing that, you can't be doing something else. Every action you take excludes a range of alternative possibilities.

PART I:
PREPARING THE WAY FOR BALANCE AND VARIETY

To prepare the way for creating a balanced and varied needs circle, think about the people and activities you would like in your life that are not there now. Some of you have TOO MANY people and activities in your lives and consequently don't have time for what you really want. Some of you don't have ENOUGH people and activities and consequently are not able to meet your needs with balance and variety.

On the surface these problems look different. However, the basic problem is the same:

Not enough thought has been given to figuring out what YOU really want to meet all four of your needs. And not enough action has been taken to get what you want.

You may recall that back in the target practice for Chapter 2 you compiled a list of your wishes. Take a look at that wish list now and think about your wishes. But remember: THINKING alone will not create more variety in your life. Thinking is only a start.

Only by DOING SOMETHING DIFFERENT will you vary how you meet your needs and increase your options.

Remember also that you only have 24 hours in the day to meet your physical and mental needs. That's not much time.

Now, think clearly about what you really want.

Take a close look at the needs circle you did on page 115. Ask yourself if all of the activities and people in your circle are fulfilling your needs. Ask yourself if you are in turn helping the people in your life meet their needs. Now think about making the adjustments that will benefit everyone involved. That may mean spending less or no time with some people and more time with others. Or you may have to cut down on some activities in order to spend more time on your favorite ones.

The exercise on the next page will help you find the right balance and variety.

If your problem is that you don't have enough fulfilling activities and people in your life, go straight to the "Action Indexes" starting on page 141. Then fill in the exercise on the next page with the people and activities you would like in your life.

DECISION TIME:

Write down which activities and people YOU want to cut down on. This is not easy. These decisions are hard but necessary if you want to be happier with your life. BE HONEST.

ACTIVITIES:

PEOPLE:

SECOND THOUGHTS:

Look at your list above. There may be a person or an activity that you do not want to take out of your life even though you have faced the fact that the person or activity is not meeting your needs. A solution is to think of ways the activity or person might be more need-fulfilling, then DO what it takes to make that happen.

(More on this in the next TARGET PRACTICE on "strengthening your relationships.")

*Every individual needs revolution, inner division,
overthrow of existing order and renewal.*
        – C.G. JUNG

There is only one person who can decide if you are meeting your needs in the long run. There is only one person who knows what other people and activities will meet your needs. **YOU.**

Your most well-meaning parent, spouse, friend, lover or child can't do this job for you. You are on your own. You have to decide. By being true to yourself, your pictures.

Think about this:

Your third grade
teacher said
you had a problem
with math.
You gave up on
math, and you forever
eliminated two-thirds
of the jobs
available in
this world.
Somebody
decided the
Navy needed
a cook.
After your
hitch, you opened
a restaurant.
Mother was a nurse.
Now you are.
Because *you* want
to be there?
Think about it.
Maybe you
ought to be
somewhere else.
Maybe it's
not too late
to figure out
where, and how
to get there.

PART II:

CREATING A BALANCED AND VARIED WANTS CIRCLE

Look at your circle again. Decide what changes you want to make. Which relationships and activities do you want to add to have more balance and variety? What do you have that you want to keep?

Put what you already have and want to keep in the center of each quadrant.

Put what you want to add on the outside of the quadrant. (See example.) Refer to your wish list on page 68. Think hard about what would make you happier.

If you are having trouble with this, look at the "Action Index" at the end of this chapter for some suggestions for meeting each need. Find the ones that you need help with and do the exercise. Then complete your circle on the following page.

EXAMPLE:

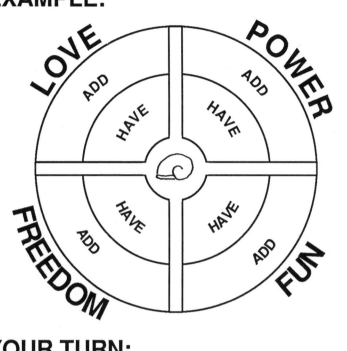

YOUR TURN:

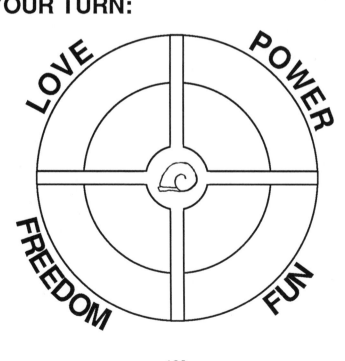

139

ACTIONS SPEAK LOUDER
THAN WORDS...

Now that you have finished your needs circle, think about which "want" you are going to start with and figure out what you must do to get what you want.

Answer this question. What will I DO today to start getting what I want to add to my life?

The **ACTION INDEX** (one for each need) is included in case you need some help in meeting your needs with more variety. They are only suggestions. One of them might remind you of something you wanted to try but have forgotten.

If you need help in this area, you can read the action index for the need you are having the most trouble with, or all of them.

REMEMBER: You can't always get what you want, but you CAN always get what you need.

YOU MEET YOUR NEEDS THROUGH ACTIVITIES YOU DO WITH YOURSELF AND OTHER PEOPLE.

YOU WILL BE HAPPIER WITH YOUR LIFE IF THE ACTIVITIES AND PEOPLE IN IT MEET MORE THAN ONE NEED, PREFERABLY ALL OF THEM.

ACTION
INDEX I

WHERE TO LOOK TO CREATE MORE LOVE AND BELONGING IN YOUR LIFE

❶ Look at your intimate relationships, with your-self, your spouse, family (parents, brothers, sisters, children, uncles, aunts, cousins), lovers, close friends, old friends. Ask yourself these questions:

• Have I been spending time alone getting to know myself and what I want, or have I been "running around" so much I have lost touch with myself?

• Have I made an effort to truly get to know these people, or have I been satisfied with not-so-intimate relationships?

• Is there someone I would like to know better whose needs I could meet and who could meet my needs?

• Is there someone I used to know and like whom I haven't seen for a long time?

❷ Think of your casual acquaintances. Would you like to know any of these people better but you haven't made the effort? Perhaps you have been hesitant to take the first step.

❸ Find a group to join. There are as many groups as there are subjects in the world. They usually welcome anyone interested in doing what the rest of the group is doing. For example: book clubs, sports teams, protest movements, political campaigns, stamp collectors, chess clubs, rock collectors, musical groups, boating clubs, skiing clubs, poetry clubs, writing clubs, health clubs, etc.

Ask yourself: Can I think of a group I would be interested in that would add some variety to my life?

❹ Although you may not think of work as a way to meet your need to belong, there are usually people there who are interested in the same things you are. They can be a great source of belonging in your life. Think about your co-workers, clients, even your boss. Could you have better relationships with these people that would add variety to your life?

❺ There are doctors, preachers, priests, counselors, therapists, holistic health professionals, etc. who can both help meet your need for belonging and show you how you can help yourself.

DONT GIVE UP

ACTION
INDEX II

WHERE TO LOOK TO CREATE MORE POWER AND RECOGNITION IN YOUR LIFE

❶ Look for ways that you can receive more recognition from yourself and others. Joining a club that recognizes or develops your special talents may be one way to do this. Or, perhaps you've always wanted to be the guest editor in the newspaper. Go ahead, try it.

A way to get more power in your life is to become more competent at doing something. This doesn't necessarily mean a job. It could be sports, cooking, ANYTHING.

For example:
Tod learned gourmet cooking. He says he gets a great deal of power when he knows just the right spice to add to a recipe.

Jessica swims competitively. Even though she doesn't always come in first, she receives recognition from being on the team. She also feels competent when she perfects a stroke.

Sam changed jobs even though no raise was involved. His pay was the same, but he was in a position of authority.

❷ Another way to get more power is to be in charge of SOMETHING, anything. If you do

143

any job well you will meet your own need for power and you will most likely get some recognition from someone.

There are lots of events requiring people to take charge. Look around your community. It will be hard work, but worth it if you're a little lacking in the power area of your circle.

❸ Having impact on people is a way to gain power. When you can have a positive influence on someone you feel powerful. Have you ever thought about being a "big brother" or "big sister"? Many successful people do this.

ACTION
INDEX III

WHERE TO LOOK TO CREATE MORE FUN AND PLEASURE IN YOUR LIFE

❶ Look for new things to learn. Learning can give you an enormous amount of pleasure. Using your mind is a powerful and sometimes neglected way to have fun.

Obviously many kinds of recreation are fun. Perhaps you used to do more things for fun than you do now. Ask yourself: What did I do for fun in the past?.

❷ Here is a list of fun things that Jean and I came up with. Maybe some of these things that are fun for us would be fun for you. Maybe NOT.

- wear something unusual or "dress up"
- buy an ice cream cone
- call a friend long distance
- eat breakfast "out"
- hear a joke, learn a joke, tell a joke
- window shop
- go to the Thrift Shop
- make a special dinner in the middle of the week
- play golf
- go to an aerobics class
- make popcorn and watch a favorite TV show
- play games
- ride in a hot air balloon
- sit in a hot tub
- go to the park
- have a picnic in the living room and watch a movie
- surprise someone with something nice
- take a trip
- go dancing
- notice the "view"
- be spontaneous

If you can find anything on this list that you like to do, but haven't done lately, add it to your wants.

ACTION
INDEX IV

WHERE TO LOOK TO CREATE MORE
FREEDOM IN YOUR LIFE

Freedom is tricky. It takes some thought to meet this need.

❶ Think about how you make decisions. Are you putting them off, or are you making them when you need to?

❷ When you CREATE something, you will have a sense of freedom. When was the last time you created something? A flower arrangement, tree house, piece of jewelry. Try to design something and then make it.

❸ Another place to look for freedom is in your movement. You can move more and feel freer. No kidding. Dance tonight in the privacy of your home and see how free you feel. Are you exercising enough? Add exercise to your life and you will have more freedom.

❹ Allow yourself some FREE time. This is time when you are not supposed to be doing anything. Allow yourself to be spontaneous and do whatever you want to for a half hour. Start small.

❺ Make choices about your daily life, and your future life. Even the smallest choice will add to your sense of freedom. Do you always eat the same breakfast? Make the choice to eat something different tomorrow.

❻ Gardens give people a sense of freedom, even though it is hard work to have one.

RELATIONSHIPS

⑥ STRENGTHEN YOUR RELATIONSHIPS

You meet your needs through other people. It's tempting to pretend that you don't need others in order to be happy. But it's not true. You need to have at least one person in your life whom you care about and who cares about you.

But since each person has their own set of wants (we all have the same needs), it is inevitable that there are conflicts.

It's easy to name the people in your life who pose problems for you. But knowing just what to do about them is not so simple. That's because often they happen to be the same people who help make you happy by fulfilling at least some of your needs.

That's why you need to strengthen your relationships with the people who are important to you.

YOU MEET YOUR NEEDS THROUGH OTHER PEOPLE AND OTHER PEOPLE MEET THEIR NEEDS THROUGH YOU. THIS TAKES WORK.

WHO ARE YOUR PROBLEM PEOPLE?

WHO ARE THE PROBLEM PEOPLE IN MY LIFE?

Most of the problem people in your life are people you know well. They are the people whom you WANT to meet your needs. Problem people are usually your husband, wife, boy/girl friend, children, parents, teachers, or boss.

(Actually, the casual acquaintances in your life rarely cause you problems.)

You want to be close to these people and sometimes have great difficulty doing this. A definition of "close to another person" is that you meet their needs, and they meet yours.

SO WHY DO I HAVE PROBLEMS WITH PEOPLE I LOVE?

Loved ones can pose problems because they don't meet your needs in the ways YOU want them to meet your needs.

(Maybe that's because you're not meeting their needs in the ways they want them met!)

The picture in your head of what your son should be doing is different from what he in fact is doing.

151

WHY DO CONFLICTS ARISE?

When you are trying to meet your needs with another person there is usually some conflict. Each of you has different pictures of how you want your needs met.

Conflicts can arise over something as simple as what to have for dinner or as complex as where to live. A conflict that many couples face today is whose career is "most important." If you have faced this problem or a similiar one, you know that "most important" is usually dependent on whose viewpoint is being taken.

PAY ATTENTION
WHEN YOU HEAR PHRASES LIKE:

"You're wrong."

"That's a stupid thing to want."

"I don't believe you're real."

"You always have to be right."

"Your mind is made up."

"You never listen to me."

"You wouldn't understand,
even if I told you."

You will certainly get a signal that tells you that you are not getting what you want. Understand that you are not seeing the other person's pictures, or they are not seeing yours.

At this point you can make a decision. Do you want to figure out a way for both of you to get some of what you want, or do you want to argue? This is a CRITICAL question. Many people choose to argue, to be miserable, to try to make the other person feel guilty. Or they choose to criticize the other person or themselves.

When dealing with the people you are close to, you choose behaviors with a strong feeling component to get what you want because they work well, at least in the short run. You can usually get what you want if you cry, or whine, or tell the person he doesn't really care about you.

WHY DO I USE MY FEELINGS WITH THOSE I CARE ABOUT?

You have learned that certain actions will bring forth certain feelings in other people. You have learned what to say when you want to meet another person's needs. When people get what they want, they have positive internal signals. Conversely, you know what to say when you don't want to meet their needs or give them what they want. When people don't get what they want, they experience negative internal signals.

As a small child, you watched those around you. You learned that saying or doing certain things influenced people to give you what you wanted. You learned that smiling and hugging and complimenting helped you get your needs met. Begging, pleading, clinging, and crying probably worked some of the time to get you what you wanted. Withdrawing, sulking, and not answering controlled those around you to give you what you wanted.

Just as you use these behaviors with a strong feeling component to influence others to give you what you want, they use them to control you. How have you taught the people you love to control you? What do you let work on you? Guilt? Threats?

Positive or negative controlling behaviors that have a strong emotional component don't work on inanimate objects. A car doesn't start because we yell at it. A chair won't turn around when we don't answer. Strong human behaviors only work on people.

However, these behaviors don't get you what you want in the long term: a good relationship. The reason for this is simple. Every time you use a controlling behavior on another person, you are interfering with that person meeting her needs. Eventually, she will feel manipulated.

Manipulation is one person meeting his needs at the expense of another. You have violated the need for freedom when you use a controlling behavior on another person. It may "look better" if you use a positive behavior (flattery), but the results are usually the same. For example, if I tell you how wonderful you are and then ask for a favor, you will not believe that I meant what I said. I did it to get what I wanted.

Most of your relationships will be better if you eliminate controlling behaviors.

HOW CAN I DO BETTER WITH PEOPLE I CARE ABOUT?

There are three main behaviors that you can use with problem people in your life. They are ACTION behaviors.

❶ SAY WHAT YOU WANT

The first is to SAY WHAT YOU WANT. In order for another person to meet your needs he must know how you want your needs met. You may now believe that if a person truly loves you she will KNOW what you want.

THIS IS NOT TRUE.

The only way for other people to know what you want is for YOU to tell them.

Valentine's Day is a great time to see the faith so many people have in mind reading.

Men and women have different pictures about Valentine's Day. This probably has to do with the fact that women have a picture of GETTING and men have a picture of GIVING. (It is also important to add that many men believe that Valentine's Day is a capitalist plot.)

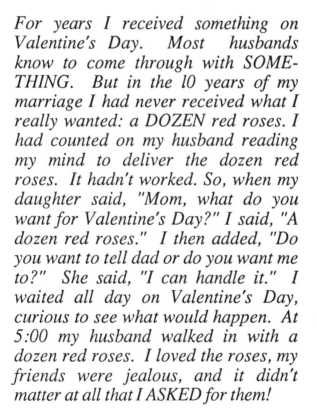

For years I received something on Valentine's Day. Most husbands know to come through with SOMETHING. But in the 10 years of my marriage I had never received what I really wanted: a DOZEN red roses. I had counted on my husband reading my mind to deliver the dozen red roses. It hadn't worked. So, when my daughter said, "Mom, what do you want for Valentine's Day?" I said, "A dozen red roses." I then added, "Do you want to tell dad or do you want me to?" She said, "I can handle it." I waited all day on Valentine's Day, curious to see what would happen. At 5:00 my husband walked in with a dozen red roses. I loved the roses, my friends were jealous, and it didn't matter at all that I ASKED for them!

Saying what you want takes a lot of the guess work out of your relationships. It is scary to say what you want. You run the risk of the other person not wanting to give it. BUT there is a greater risk in not ever getting what you want. If you want to be happy, tell the people around you what you want. Don't forget to ask them what they want, too. You are NOT a mind reader.

LOVE does not mean reading minds.

❷ COMPROMISE AND NEGOTIATE

The second action behavior you can use with problem people is to compromise and negotiate. Most people know about compromising and negotiating but rarely use these skills with the people they are close to. You are much more likely to use such skills at work, or on a volunteer job, than at home.

You are much more likely to use behaviors with a strong feeling component on the people you are close to and especially with the problem people in your life. When you are frustrated, and when you think nothing will help, you use your ineffective and band-aid behaviors to try to control other people.

You are also more likely to use your ineffective and band-aid behaviors on someone you have "fallen in love with" because it is so surprising when things start to fall apart.

When you fall in love, you have the illusion that one person can meet all your needs. This is probably because you fall in love with someone who has pictures that are very similar to yours. (Or at least, on first glance it looks like your pictures are the same.) This state doesn't usually last. So be ready to negotiate how the two of you can adapt to unexpected changes.

❸ SAY YES

A third action behavior you can use with people you love is to

SAY YES AS MUCH AS POSSIBLE.

If you practice the fine art of saying "yes" you will be amazed at how many problems disappear. This is especially effective with children, of whatever age.

Think about it: Many times you say NO to a child not because there is a good reason, but because it is easier to say no than to say yes. You think that by saying no you will save yourself some trouble. Usually, saying no causes trouble because when you say no, you are saying YOU CAN'T HAVE WHAT YOU WANT.

If you say YES, but we have to work out the details, you usually will save yourself a lot of grief. You will also be raising a child who is more responsible than one who hears NO a lot.

However, if you have to say NO, mean it. Sometimes there are good reasons to say no. "Can I go to a rock concert in Atlanta, three hours away by car with my 16-year-old friend driving?" "No, it's too dangerous." At this point your teenager will beg, plead, whine. Don't change your mind. If you say no, mean it.

My parents were great believers in the Yes Theory of child rearing. They said yes a lot more than they said no. (They said no when someone could get hurt.) I was responsible (most of the time).

When I was a freshman in college I decided I wanted to leave my nice safe all-girls school to go to France for a year with some classmates. Of course, we didn't want to go on an already-established school program; we wanted to plan the trip ourselves. We figured we'd use the money we would have spent on tuition for a year to pay for the entire trip.

We were sure that our parents would say no. But when I asked my mother she said, "What a wonderful idea!" My father guessed our plans and approved before I even explained it all to him. And to our amazement the other parents said yes also.

What this meant was that we had to take complete responsibility for the trip. We had to study French, make a budget, write in French for a place to live and find an inexpensive way of getting to Europe. It was work. But planning and carrying out our dream was one of the best learning experiences of my college career.

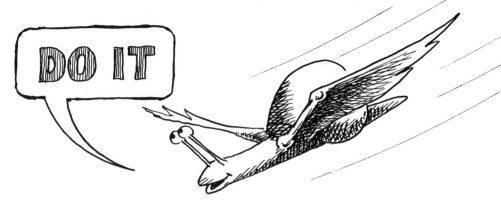

PART I:
LEARN TO SAY WHAT YOU WANT

You may care a lot about the problem people in your life, but you don't seem to be able to really talk to them. Perhaps you used to talk, but now you don't. Frequently problems begin because you believe the person knows what you want but they just aren't giving it to you. This could be a spouse, child, parent, anyone close to you.

You have a strong belief that this person can read your mind, or anticipate your wants. Often others don't know what you want because you haven't told them. Most of us HOPE the others can figure out what we want.

If you can believe that NO ONE but you truly understands what you want and exactly how you want it, you can be a lot happier with your life.

Now that you know what you want, tell the important people in your life and encourage them to tell you what they want. That is the only chance you have of getting what you want to meet your needs, and vice versa. This is called communication. When you have problems with a person you usually say, "We just don't communicate." Not communicating is another way of saying "I don't know what she wants."

163

A MAJOR OBSTACLE IN TELL-
ING OTHERS WHAT YOU WANT:
CRITICISM

It is very hard to tell another person what you want if you believe that you will be criticized. There is a very good reason for this. Your pictures are your image of what would be ideal for you. If another person laughs at them, or lets you know that you will never be able to get what you want, then you will have negative internal signals. When you can't get what you need, you view yourself as a failure.

BEWARE

When you criticize another person's pictures it is usually because their pictures interfere with YOUR pictures.

Very often teenagers shut down communication with their parents because they are criticized constantly. Parents refuse to listen to what the teenager wants because it is often not what the parent wants for the teenager. However, if you criticize and shut down communication, then there is little or no chance for a better relationship. The teenager will continue to be a problem.

IF YOU WANT TO GET ALONG
BETTER WITH PROBLEM PEOPLE,
DON'T CRITICIZE THEM.

TARGET PRACTICE

❶ A person I am having a problem with:

❷ Something(s) I want from this person that I'm not getting:

❸ When will I tell this person what I REALLY want?

My experience has been that most of the time when you tell someone close to you what you really want, they will try to help you get it. Sometimes this involves compromise and negotiation because for a relationship to work, one person can't have everything he or she wants all the time.

MORE PRACTICE:

Another way to practice giving up mind reading is to think of the next special occasion coming up in your life. Is it your birthday, your spouse's birthday, Christmas, Valentine's Day? Pick one.

❶ Tell one person close to you what you REALLY want. It doesn't HAVE to be a material present. Many times the present you really want is to spend more time with the person.   Let him know this.

❷ Ask a problem person what she wants from you on this special occasion. See if you can open up communication by listening instead of criticizing.

THINK ABOUT THIS:

Use this process of saying what you want and listening to others' wants not only for special occasions but for bigger, life-long wants. Mary Lou was unhappy for years because her husband wanted a big, expensive house and worked himself sick to get it. She wanted a simpler house and lifestyle but was afraid to tell him. When she finally got up the nerve to let him know, he was relieved. He thought SHE wanted the big house and took on the pressure to please her.

PART II:
LEARN TO COMPROMISE AND NEGOTIATE

It's probably easy for you, like most people, to see that someone else is not meeting your needs.

It's easy to criticize others' faults and shortcomings. But doing so diverts you from the difficult work of seeing how YOU aren't meeting the other person's needs. Take a look at what you are doing to cause the problem.

BUT I THOUGHT YOU WERE THE PROBLEM

CHANGING YOURSELF IS HARD WORK.

CHANGING ANOTHER PERSON IS IMPOSSIBLE.

One way to identify problem people is to listen to yourself. When you are saying or thinking to yourself: "If only he would

_____

THEN I would be happier," you have a problem.

When you hear yourself saying this, realize that you have a problem. Knowing that you have a problem and facing it, is the first step in finding a solution.

 **TAKE AIM**

Name a problem person in your life:

_____

Ask this person if she or he would like to have a better relationship with you, since you would like to have a better one with her or him.

If the answer is YES go to activity
A: WORK IT OUT TOGETHER

If the answer is NO go to activity
B: DO WHAT YOU CAN ALONE

A: WORK IT OUT TOGETHER

THE GOAL: Your goal in the following exercise is to find out how much each of you wants to give and how much each of you wants to get.

Trying to find a balance in the relationship is the key.

❶ Each of you think about your basic needs: LOVE • POWER • FUN • FREEDOM. What do you want from each other in relation to these needs?

❷ Discuss "maintenance" issues in your relationship. Talk about the last time each need was met and plan for an update. Make a plan to add at least one activity that you both enjoy doing together.

❸ Talk about your pictures in detail. Compare and contrast. Plan how you can compromise and negotiate, and/or match each other's pictures. Here are some examples. My picture
of: a family vacation
a romantic evening
a good wife/husband/mother/daughter/
son/ boy or girl friend
a well-run household
this relationship

When you describe your picture that means what would be ideal for YOU.

When your problem person describes his picture, that means what would be ideal for him.

❹ The last step is to see what each of you can LIVE WITH. No one can get everything she wants. Not if you plan to live with other people.

Life is not as straightforward when you have to think of others, but it can be happier if you learn to compromise and negotiate.

B. DO WHAT YOU CAN ALONE

THE GOAL: The goal here is for you to decide whether you can or want to remain in a relationship that is not what you want. Many people do stay in marriages, or cope with difficult parents and children, even when the other people are not interested in compromising or negotiating. In other words, there are many situations where people hang in – whatever the reason.

If your problem person is not willing to work on the problem there are several things you can DO.

❶ You can choose to change yourself and become more need satisfying to that person, so she can see what having needs met means. You may believe that you have done this, you have already given all you have to give. And you may have. If so, move on to the next step, while still trying to be need fulfilling to the problem person.

❷ You can choose to meet more of your own needs by adding new activities to your life (see the Action Indexes, page 141). You may have focused so much on the problem person that you are not doing many of the activities you used to enjoy.

❸ You can decide the minimum you want from the person. What exactly will you settle for? We do this in all our relationships. Tell the other person what you have decided and give him a chance to give it to you.

❹ If all of the above do not improve the relationship then you must ask yourself the hard question. "Is staying in this relationship interfering with my ability to be happy?" If you have tried to meet your needs in the relationship, and it clearly blocks you, then you have little choice. You cannot stay strong and be happy and satisfied with your life if there are people in it who don't care about you. If a problem person really cares about you, she will be willing to try to work it out if you are unhappy.

If she doesn't want to work it out after you have tried everything then your conclusion must be that she doesn't truly care about you.

Most of the time this is a very painful fact to face. If you are in this situation, talk to a friend or a therapist. Don't face this alone.

❺ Leave the relationship. This is a difficult step to take, but when another person interferes with your meeting your needs, you must take it. You probably know a person who has stayed in a relationship that prevented him from meeting his needs. It is a tragic situation to watch, and a worse one to be in.

If there is a problem person in your life and that person refuses to change, you must change yourself by leaving the relationship and choosing a new, need-fulfilling one so you can be strong and happy. It is not even necessary to add another person. Try developing your relationship with yourself.

YOU MIGHT FIND THE PROBLEM PERSON HAS BEEN SUCH AN ENERGY DRAIN THAT LIVING WITHOUT HIM GIVES YOU AN ENORMOUS AMOUNT OF ENERGY TO MEET YOUR NEEDS.

WHAT IF THE PROBLEM PERSON WON'T GO AWAY?

OR

WHAT IF I AM RESPONSIBLE FOR HIM?

If you are really certain that you HAVE to break the relationship, you can do it. You may have to be persistent with someone you have allowed to run all over you. But if you let him know it's over, eventually he'll get the message. I know people who have called the police to convince a problem person to leave. It's not easy, but other people do it, and so can you.

REMEMBER:
YOU NEED PEOPLE IN YOUR LIFE, BUT NOT ANY ONE PERSON.

PART III:
MAKE SOMEONE'S DAY

It's hard work to strengthen your significant relationships, but well worth the effort. One way to strengthen relationships is to catch people in the act of doing something right (in your opinion).

Practice this by complimenting people you don't know so well. This is need-fulfilling both for you and for the other person.

It will also help you find "positives" in the people close to you.

I made _____ 's day
by

THE WASHINGTON POST

Take a look at what well-known humorist Art Buchwald has to say on the subject:

YOU JUST WINKED AT A VERY PLAIN LOOKING WOMAN

By Art Buchwald

I was in New York the other day and rode with a friend in a taxi. When we got out my friend said to the driver, "Thank you for the ride. You did a superb job of driving."

The taxi driver was stunned for a second. Then he said: "Are you a wise guy or something?"

"No my dear man, and I'm not putting you on. I admire the way you keep cool in heavy traffic."

"Yeh," the driver said and drove off.

"What was that all about?" I asked.

"I am trying to bring love back to New York," he said. "I believe it's the only thing that can save the city."

"How can one man save New York?"

"It's not one man. I believe I have made that taxi driver's day. Suppose he has 20 fares. He's going to be nice to those 20 fares because someone was nice to him. Those fares in turn will be kinder to their employees or shopkeepers or waiters or even their own families. Eventually the good will could spread to at least 1,000 people. Now that isn't bad, is it?"

"But you're depending on it," my friend said.

"I'm aware that the system isn't fool-proof so I might deal with 10 different people today. If, out of 10, I can make three happy, then eventually I can indirectly influence the attitudes of 3,000 more."

"It sounds good on paper," I admitted, "but I'm not sure it works in practice."

"Nothing is lost if it doesn't. It didn't take any of my time to tell that man he was doing a good job. He neither received a larger tip nor a smaller tip. If it fell on deaf ears, so what? Tomorrow there will be another taxi driver whom I can try to make happy."

"You're some kind of a nut," I said.

"That shows you how cynical you have become. I have made a study of this. The thing that seems to be lacking, besides money of course, for our postal employees, is that

177

no one tells people who work for the post office what a good job they're doing."

"But they're not doing a good job because they feel no one cares if they do or not. Why shouldn't someone say a kind word to them?"

We were walking past a structure in the process of being built and passed five workmen eating their lunch. My friend stopped. "That's a magnificent job you men have done. It must be difficult and dangerous work."

The five men eyed my friend suspiciously.

"When will it be finished?"

"June," a man grunted.

"Ah. That really is impressive. You must be very proud."

We walked away. I said to him, "I haven't seen anyone like you since 'The Man from La Mancha'."

"When those men digest my words, they will feel beter for it. Somehow the city will benefit from their happiness."

"But you can't do this all alone!" I protested. "You're just one man."

"The most important thing is not to get discouraged. Making people in the city become kind again is not an easy job, but if I can enlist other people in my campaign..."

"You just winked at a very plain looking woman," I said.

"Yes, I know," he replied. "And if she's a schoolteacher, her class will be in for a fantastic day." (Reprinted with permission of Art Buchwald.)

178

IMAGINATION

⑦ USE YOUR IMAGINATION

You have a resourceful imagination which generates behaviors you can use to solve problems and meet your needs. Some people call this creativity.

Your imagination can be a strong ally. Learning to use your creativity can be a big step in your pursuit of happiness.

You may think that you are not "imaginative" or "creative." On the other hand, you may be imaginative and creative at work or in the arts, but your personal life is a mess. You don't use your creativity to solve your own problems.

Learning to use your creativity is not as hard as it might seem. Certainly, at some time in your life you have gotten a "far out" idea of how to solve a problem, and it worked. Or perhaps you made something you had no idea how to make.

In other words, you surprised yourself. When you surprise yourself you know that you are using your creativity. You say, "It just came to me out of the blue." Actually, it didn't come out of the blue, it came out of YOU, out of your imagination.

Tapping into your creativity is easier than you think. You probably use it more than you think you do.

The first principle to remember is that your imagination will give you lots of crazy ideas. Some of them may even scare you. This is the system that has kept us alive over the centuries. The first person who swam probably used this system when she found herself in water over her head and didn't know what to do. She started moving her hands and legs, and presto, she was swimming!

Now, when the system gives you a "crazy" idea you probably reject it and say, "I can't do that." When you do this, it stops the system from working.

The trick is to listen to the crazy ideas and not be afraid of them. Your crazy ideas only become a problem when you act on them.

Frequently the idea your imagination throws out may be wild but part of the idea might be workable. Brainstorming is a way that people tap their creativity. The chief rule in brainstorming is that you say anything that comes to mind. Another rule is that there is no criticism. When you are criticized your creativity stops working.

Corporations have used the technique of brainstorming for many years to solve "unsolvable" problems. Here's a story I heard about something that happened in Canada. The telephone company was having a large problem with the wires icing up and breaking in the middle of winter. A team of engineers was called in to solve the problem and they decided to start by brainstorming. One of the suggestions in the brainstorming session was to have birds fly above the wires during snow storms because the motion of their wings would keep the snow from sticking to the wires. Obviously, this is a ridiculous idea. Would the company hire the birds? Would the birds want to fly in the snowstorm? BUT this creative, imaginative idea, ridiculous as it sounds, held the beginning of the final solution. Believe it or not, the solution was to have helicopters fly above the wires during snowstorms to keep the lines free. It worked.

BRAINSTORMING
IT WON'T HURT
IT MIGHT HELP

If this technique can work for corporations, why don't you use it in your life? Because you don't think of using it, and it sometimes scares you. But, if you understand it, you can make it work for you.

Here's an example of when my creative system worked. It happened years ago, but I remember the moment as if it was yesterday.

I was working in a job that I wanted to quit but didn't have a good reason to leave. I had been thinking about the problem for some time when quite suddenly one day – "out of the blue" – came this thought: If you just take off your clothes and run down the street nude, they will fire you from the job. (I was a mental health counselor, and obviously it wouldn't do for me to be running around nude.)

I thought about this for a moment, amazed that I would have such an idea. Then I said to myself, "That won't do; come up with another idea." I then realized that I could leave if I did so responsibly. I didn't HAVE to have any other reason. Although this seems obvious now, at the time it was a very creative thought because I had convinced myself that I had to offer a REASON for leaving.

I then resigned, saying that I would leave when a replacement for me could be found.

The second principle that helps in using your imagination or creativity is to believe that:

THERE IS A SOLUTION TO EVERY PROBLEM, NO MATTER HOW DIFFICULT THE PROBLEM MAY SEEM.

YOU HAVE THE SOLUTION WITHIN YOURSELF.

If you believe that the solutions to your problems are outside yourself you will have a hard time being happy.

You have probably heard that the solutions to your problems are inside you. When I first heard this, I said,"WHERE?"

Now it is clear that the solutions to problems are in your imagination, if you look.

The third principle to remember is that your creative system is working all the time to try to help you get what you want.

It is your choice. Will you consciously pay attention to what your imagination is telling you or will you ignore it?

Your creative system is NOT designed to be idle. It is always trying to help you meet your needs. You can continue living an unsatisfying life, but your system will not turn off.

If you don't meet your needs, you will get signals telling you something is wrong. Your ways of acting on your signals, whether conscious or unconscious, will become increasingly drastic. Maybe your occasional headaches will become chronic; your irritability will grow into open hostility; your occasional glass of wine will develop into a drinking habit.

THAT'S THE BAD NEWS.

But the same system that generates headaches, hostility, depression and drug abuse has the creativity to give you positive, effective ways to meet your needs.

THAT'S THE GOOD NEWS.

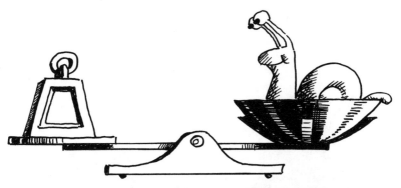

BALANCE YOUR BEHAVIORS

When your creativity goes to work for you, you will think about many different behaviors you can use to get what you want. This could be to get what you want from yourself or from other people.

You might think of a "doing" behavior, or a "thinking" behavior which will get you what you want. These are your most effective behaviors but sometimes you will want to use a "doing" or "thinking" behavior with a strong feeling or physical component. An example of this would be when a child runs in the street and a car is coming you would not rationally say, "Please get out of the street." You would scream, "Move, get out of the way!" This behavior with it's urgent feeling is THE behavior to use in this case.

People who tap their creativity have a wide variety of behaviors available to them, and they use them. Good parents, teachers and bosses use their creativity in their relationships with their children, students and employees. Sometimes they are rigid; sometimes they are flexible. They are not stuck with one main behavior. They use their imaginations, and their relationships are remarkably better than others. They understand that our behaviors are there to help us get what we want and to help us give other people what they want.

**IF YOU CAN IMAGINE IT
YOU CAN ACHIEVE IT
IF YOU CAN DREAM IT
YOU CAN BECOME IT**

PART I:
GAINING ACCESS TO YOUR IMAGINATION

The fastest way to gain access to your imagination is to do some activity every day that will put you in touch with your creativity.

The activity could be anything from meditating to jogging to hot baths, anything that allows you at least 20 to 30 minutes of time just for you. Primarily it should be an activity that you enjoy and that makes you feel good about yourself when you've finished doing it. You are proud that you have done it. Although it sounds strange, if you are a busy mother, taking a 20 minute uninterrupted hot bath is something to be proud of.

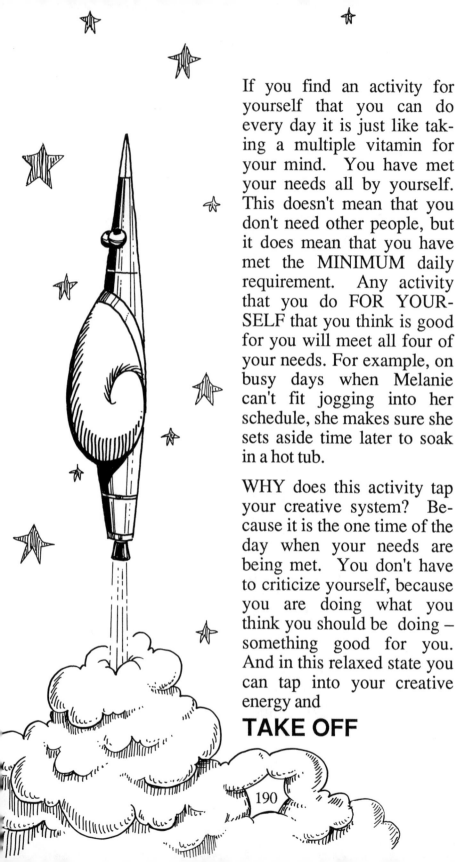

If you find an activity for yourself that you can do every day it is just like taking a multiple vitamin for your mind. You have met your needs all by yourself. This doesn't mean that you don't need other people, but it does mean that you have met the MINIMUM daily requirement. Any activity that you do FOR YOURSELF that you think is good for you will meet all four of your needs. For example, on busy days when Melanie can't fit jogging into her schedule, she makes sure she sets aside time later to soak in a hot tub.

WHY does this activity tap your creative system? Because it is the one time of the day when your needs are being met. You don't have to criticize yourself, because you are doing what you think you should be doing — something good for you. And in this relaxed state you can tap into your creative energy and

TAKE OFF

190

TARGET PRACTICE

I will spend 20 minutes to a half hour each day doing:

I will start this activity on _____ .

I do not know which activity I want to do each day, but I will start thinking about which one I want to choose and start by doing one tomorrow. What I will do tomorrow is:

PART II:
BRAINSTORM AND BALANCE YOUR BEHAVIORS

You can brainstorm by yourself to solve problems in your life. The only thing necessary is time to yourself to do this. It won't work if you are in a hurry or are under pressure. A good time to brainstorm is after you have finished your special daily activity.

When you brainstorm it's a good idea to write down what you think about. It's not entirely necessary, but you might lose some good ideas if you don't write them down.

 **TAKE AIM**

Think about a problem you are having now that you would like to solve:

Ask yourself this question: Have I balanced my behaviors in relationship to this problem or have I been stuck on one behavior. What behavior am I using now to solve the problem?

Now brainstorm: Here are all the solutions I can think of, no matter how crazy or far out:

Now, pick one and see if you think it would work, or if you could modify it to make it work:

PART III:
THE GRAND FINALE

You probably have a lot of handy excuses and good reasons why changing your life "at this time" would be too difficult, risky, unwise, etc. You know your own excuses. You would like to be happier, but you do nothing but THINK about it.

When you THINK about how you would like your life to be, but DO nothing to get what you want, you are essentially making yourself weaker. This is one way that you are "your own worst enemy." You are criticizing yourself. Every time you criticize yourself you take away from your mental strength.

IF YOU ARE IN THE PROCESS OF BECOMING THE PERSON YOU WANT TO BE, YOU WILL BE HAPPIER.

Here is a very good question that I learned from a friend:

How would the person you want to be handle this situaton?

The situation could be anything: losing weight, dealing with a problem person, making a move, changing jobs, ANYTHING.

If you are not handling the situation the way you would like to be handling it, then you will not be happy with yourself or your life.

 **TAKE AIM**

❶ To become the person you want to be, the person you picture in your mind's eye, START SMALL.

You'd like to change overnight. But, you probably won't, so the faster you can get rid of that idea, the happier you will be.

You are getting a SIGNAL that tells you that you are not getting what you want, but you are doing nothing about it right now.

The problem or situation that I would be handling differently if I were the person I want to be is:

BECOMING THE PERSON YOU WANT TO BE

❷ Pick one small action you can take to start getting what you want to meet your needs. If you complete this action, you will move closer to being the person you want to be. You will, as a consequence, be HAPPIER.

The action I will take to handle this situation the way I want is:

BEING HAPPIER IS POSSIBLE

IF EVERY TIME YOU FEEL AN INTERNAL SIGNAL YOU ACT TO GET WHAT YOU WANT.

IF YOU HANDLE THE SITUATION LIKE THE PERSON YOU WANT TO BE WOULD HANDLE IT.

IF YOU MOVE TOWARD MEETING YOUR NEEDS WITHOUT STOPPING OTHER PEOPLE FROM MEETING THEIR NEEDS.

If you want to be happier you have to ACT.

REMEMBER:

SIGNAL THINK ACT

THE END

Guides to In Pursuit of Happiness

❖ Good, E. Perry, *The "Happy Hour" Guide*. Chapel Hill: New View Publications, 1989.

10 group sessions for adolescents and adults.

❖ Haberman, Delores, *Teacher's Guide to In Pursuit of Happiness*. Chapel Hill: New View Publications, 1992.

Activities and ideas to teach middle and high school students about themselves, their behavior, and how to pursue happiness.

Further Readings

Ford, Edward, *Love Guaranteed*. New York: Brandt Publishing, 1987.

Glasser, William, *Reality Therapy*. New York: HarperCollins, 1969.

Glasser, William, *Positive Addiction*. New York: HarperCollins, 1972.

Glasser, William, *Control Theory*. New York: HarperCollins, 1984.

Good, E. Perry, *Helping Kids Help Themselves*. Chapel Hill: New View Publications, 1992.

Gossen, Diane Chelsom, *Restitution: Restructuring School Discipline*. Chapel Hill: New View Publications, 1992.

Sullo, Robert A., *Teach Them to Be Happy*. Chapel Hill: New View Publications, 1989.

Wubbolding, Robert E., *Using Reality Therapy*. New York: HarperCollins, 1986.

Beyond Further Readings
(The following books are theoretical in nature.)

Glasser, William, *Stations of the Mind*. New York: HarperCollins, 1981.

Powers, William T., *Behavior: The Control of Perception*. Chicago: Aldine Publishing Co., 1973.

Writer E. Perry Good and artist Jeffrey Hale met 20 years ago while working at a San Francisco film studio.

Perry has taught disadvantaged youth, counseled runaways and instructed mental health professionals who work with teenagers and adults. She received her master's in educational anthropology from New York University, then studied and worked with Dr. William Glasser, originator of the principles of Reality Therapy. Since then, Perry has become a noted counselor, theorist and instructor in her own right. Today she is a consultant and Senior Faculty Member of Glasser's Institute for Reality Therapy. Her dynamic seminars are acclaimed by individuals, social service agencies, businesses, students, teachers, counselors and other professionals. She lives in Chapel Hill, N.C. with her husband Fred Good, an artist, and their daughter Jessica.

Internationally renowned animator Jeffrey Hale grew up in "Dreamland" the Coney Island of southern England. A graduate of the Royal College of Art in London, he has produced, directed, and animated numerous theatrical shorts, including "The Great Toy Robbery" and "Thank You Mask Man" (sound track by Lenny Bruce). His television credits include animation for commercials, specials, and "Sesame Street," with which he has been associated since the show began. His work has been exhibited and honored at film festivals around the world and he has been nominated for two Academy Awards. Today Jeffrey lives in Bynum, N.C., where he continues to contemplate snails.

Need a present for a favorite friend, relative or teenager?

To order *In Pursuit of Happiness*, use the coupon below or write to:

NEW VIEW PUBLICATIONS
P.O. Box 3021
Chapel Hill, NC 27515-3021

1-800-441-3604

✂ — .

Please send me _____ copies of *In Pursuit of Happiness* @ $11 per copy plus $3.50 shipping and handling for the first book and $1.00 s/h for each additional book. (North Carolina residents add 6% sales tax.)

MAILING ADDRESS:

NAME_____

ADDRESS_____

CITY/STATE/ZIP_____

_____ I have enclosed a check or money order made payable to NEW VIEW PUBLICATIONS in the amount of $_____.

_____ Charge my:

VISA Acc't # _____

Exp. Date ____/____/____

MasterCard Acc't # _____

Exp. Date ____/____/____ Interbank # _____

Signature:

_____

(Must be signed if using VISA/MC.)